Christ, Church & Life

TEACHER'S GUIDE

Christ, Church & Life

TEACHER'S GUIDE

Kevin Preston & Brian Davis

Gracewing

A Maryvale Book

First published in 1995

Gracewing	Maryvale Institute
Fowler Wright Books	Maryvale House
Southern Ave, Leominster	Old Oscott Hill
Herefordshire, HR6 0QF	Birmingham, B44 9AG

Gracewing Books are distributed

In New Zealand by	*In Australia by*
Catholic Supplies Ltd	Charles Paine Pty Ltd
80 Adelaide Road	8 Ferris Street
Wellington	North Parramatta
New Zealand	NSW 2151, Australia
In USA by	*In Canada by*
Morehouse Publishing	Meakin & Associates
PO Box 1321	Unit 17, 81 Auriga Drive
Harrisburg	Nepean, Ontario
PA 17105, USA	KZE 7YS, Canada

Typesetting by Reesprint, Radley, Oxon, OX14 3AJ

Printed by Cromwell Press,
Broughton Gifford, Melksham, Wiltshire, SN12 8PH

ISBN 0 85244 285 8

Contents

Foreword

This text for those engaged in teaching the syllabus on *Christianity: the Roman Catholic Tradition* from the Southern Examining Group will be much appreciated. Teachers are challenged by the new syllabus to update their own subject knowledge — this 'Guide' offers welcome indicators for personal study, as well as advice on particular key areas needing emphases for the students. It is essentially a Guide for those teaching the syllabus using the Student Text, *Christ, Church and Life*.

We owe a special debt of thanks to Father Kevin Preston who, in association with Brian Davis, produced this Teacher's Guide to *Christ, Church and Life*, the book they co-authored for the students of the syllabus. The Student Text and Teacher Guide together offer all involved in studying and teaching *Christianity: the Roman Catholic Tradition* a very substantial resource. Teachers in turn will of course bring their own expertise and creativity to making the syllabus come alive for their students.

We express our special appreciation to Gracewing / Fowler Wright, the publishers, who have worked so generously with Maryvale Institute to make this resource available for teachers and students.

J. Daniel McHugh
Director, Maryvale Institute

General Introduction

Preliminary Remarks

This Teacher's Guide contains notes on the Student Text for each of the Units of the GCSE Religious Studies Syllabus, *Christianity: The Roman Catholic Tradition*, Syllabus C of the Southern Examining Group (SEG). Except where otherwise indicated, all page references are to the Student Text, *Christ, Church and Life*.

The Syllabus

The Syllabus on which the Student Text is based is one which, as its title suggests, is concerned with the study of Christianity, especially according to the Roman Catholic Tradition. This means that it contains some elements which are distinctively Roman Catholic, and that it reflects or addresses, especially in certain areas, emphases and concerns which are distinctively, though not always exclusively, Roman Catholic. There is, however, much about it that is common to most mainstream Christian denominations. It provides an approach to Christianity based mainly upon Scripture and the Creed and upon associated elements of the classical Christian theological and moral tradition which form the common patrimony of Christendom.

In following the syllabus, pupils will study key elements of: doctrine, Scripture, liturgy, morality and Christian living. Each of the Units has its main emphasis in one or other of these areas, but each also contains elements of the others. Doctrine itself is approached in a Scriptural context, and with reference to implications for behaviour and attitudes; Scripture has implications for teaching and for conduct of life; morality flows from beliefs and doctrines, and liturgy both embodies doctrine and promotes certain moral attitudes. It is one of the aims of the Student Text to promote awareness of these interconnections.

Units 1 and 4 provide the basic doctrinal underpinning. Unit 1 deals with the basic Christian teaching on Jesus Christ: as the eternal Son of God made man, at once fully man and fully divine, who comes as the Saviour, winning for human beings, and offering to them, reconciliation with God and eternal life. It involves, as it must, the fundamental Christian doctrine of the Blessed Trinity, and deals with the classical notions of atonement, redemption etc., especially in regard to the Crucifixion and Resurrection of Jesus. It provides the basis for all else, and in the main presents a tradition common to most branches of Christianity.

Unit 4 completes the theological picture, with a view of the Church as the sign and instrument through which the achievement and teaching of Christ is proclaimed and communicated in every age. It goes on to examine the nature and constitution of the Church and the ways in which the achievement of its mission is assured and brought about. Prominently included in this is consideration of some of the Sacraments, especially the Eucharist.

Unit 2 combines a study of the heart of the Gospel according to Luke (the account of the Passion and Resurrection of Jesus) with an examination of the Liturgy of Holy Week. It ensures that all pupils study a substantial portion of one of the Gospels, and also that all study the most dramatic and significant celebrations of the liturgical year. Together with the consideration of the Eucharist in Unit 4, this forms the major item of liturgical study in the syllabus.

Unit 3 offers a choice. For those who wish to study at least the major part of one Gospel, there is the option of dealing with the Public Ministry of Jesus, according to Luke (Alternative A). When combined with the Passion and Resurrection account in Unit 2, this enables pupils to study the whole of the Gospel of Luke, apart from the Infancy narratives (i.e. all of the part of Luke which corresponds in scope to the Gospel of Mark). This is an option which many teachers will probably wish to take.

The reason for choosing Luke lies principally in its suitability as a stimulus for moral reflection, particularly because of the wealth of parables which it contains. This enables this option to function both as a Unit of Scriptural study and a Unit particularly apt for the study of basic Christian moral themes.

The alternative, 'Issues in Christian Living' (Alternative B) is for those who do not give such a high priority to the desirability of studying one Gospel, and who would like a more systematic treatment of basic moral themes and the opportunity for exploring fundamental attitudes and basic themes involved in Christian moral teaching.

Unit 5 rounds off the moral component of the syllabus by concentrating on two highly important areas of moral concern — human life and sexuality.

Order of Teaching

The Units may very well be taken in numerical order, and it is anticipated that many schools will be happy to do this. Certainly, since the Unit on Jesus Christ is so fundamental, it seems highly appropriate that it should be tackled first, and then complemented by the Unit on the Passion and Resurrection, which would appropriately fall in the term before Easter. If Unit 3 were then covered in the final term of Year 10, this would mean that the demanding Unit 4 could be allotted to the first (and usually most productive) term of the following academic year.

On the other hand, it is not essential to follow this order. Some might think that, because Unit 1 is somewhat difficult, it would be better to 'break in' pupils more gently by tackling, say, Unit 3 first of all. If Alternative A were taken, followed by Unit 2, pupils would then cover the whole of Luke consecutively in the proper order, before going on to the more systematic and 'theological' Unit 1. Some, however, might think that the Summer term was not the best time to deal with the most difficult material.

Again, there may well be a case for dealing with Unit 2 *after* Easter, when pupils will have had opportunity to witness the celebrations of Holy Week, rather than *before it*. Arguments could be advanced for practically any order, and schools are free to make up their own minds on this matter, in accordance with what seems best in their own circumstances. There is one constraint, however, which should be taken seriously. Unit 4 (The Church) is substantially dependent on the concepts and material covered in Unit 1 (Jesus Christ). Whatever order is adopted therefore, Unit 4 should not be tackled *before* Unit 1 has been completed.

Examination Structure

It will be noted that the first written paper covers Units 1, 3 and 2(a), while the second covers Units 4, 5 and 2(b). Whatever order is adopted for teaching the Units, teachers should ensure that pupils are aware of which Units 'belong' to which paper. In order to avoid confusion, especially in regard to revision, they may well wish to devise means of ensuring that notes etc. in respect of Units belonging to the first paper are in some way kept separate from those concerned with Units belonging to the second.

Some observations on the split between the two sections of Unit 2 are given in the notes on that Unit, later on in this book.

Coursework

The syllabus requires two coursework assignments. One (in connection with Unit 4) must be concerned *either* with some aspect of a non-Catholic Christian parish/community/organisation *or* with some aspect of local ecumenical activity. The other may be *either* concerned with the life and activity of a local Roman Catholic parish, or some other aspect of Roman Catholic life, as detailed on p.15 of the syllabus, *or* it may be concerned with some aspect of a topic connected with Unit 5.

Teachers should carefully peruse the regulations on coursework contained in the syllabus, and also the Support Material provided by SEG.

Some suggestions concerning coursework may be found in the notes on Units 4 and 5. Here it may be observed that coursework provides an opportunity for assessing the performance of pupils in areas which are not easily examinable in a general written paper. It gives opportunity for personal research and initiative and for consideration of the local and particular. On the whole, it would seem better for assignments to be concerned with the concrete and particular, rather than with the theoretical and general. It should also be noted that a large proportion of the marks is allotted to evaluation, and that this emphasis should therefore be reflected in the nature and wording of assignments and in the way they are tackled.

Scripture

The version of the Bible which will be used in examination papers, and the version which is used in the Student Text, is the *Revised Standard Version* (RSV). Schools may, however, themselves employ any reputable translation in teaching all or some of the Units.

With regard to texts prescribed in connection with Units 1, 3 (Alternative B), 4 and 5, it should be emphasised that ability to perform a complete exegesis of all they contain is *not* required. Candidates are only expected to be able to comment on aspects of the texts *relevant* to the theme(s) under consideration in the Unit in question. It is recommended that teachers always go over the texts first with the class, before individual or group work is set, helping to identify and highlight key expressions, ideas etc. The treatment of Scriptural passages in the Student Text, and the questions set on them, furnish a general guide as to the level of understanding that may be expected, though occasionally questions (especially in respect of Old Testament background) may be set which go beyond what might be expected in the examination. Teachers will do well to read carefully the notes at the beginning of the *Subject Content* section of the syllabus (p.19).

Student Text

The Student Text provides a structured approach to the syllabus, one which incorporates a sound treatment of the various topics, and which relates the prescribed texts to them in an appropriate way. It is not, however, meant to be a self-sufficient teaching instrument, but needs to be used in connection with the teacher's own detailed schemes of work, adapted to the needs of particular groups of pupils. It is offered as a basic resource and framework, but like all resources, needs to be adapted and used with flexibility, in accordance with individual requirements.

The Text contains a number of suggested exercises and activities (some of them printed in the margin), and the notes in this guide add others. These are not meant to be exhaustive, nor are all necessary for all pupils. Teachers will, of course, select, adapt and supplement such activities in accordance with their own judgement, and with particular needs and aptitudes of pupils in mind.

Many of the exercises consist of lists of questions. These may serve not only as a basis for individual work by pupils, but also for class or group discussion. Such discussion may often, in any case, be a profitable preliminary to individual work. The teacher will judge the best way of employing such exercises for the benefit of any specific group.

In any case, however, it is important that pupils are given plenty of opportunity to engage in questioning and discussion. This is necessary, in the first place, to promote real *understanding*. This is, of course, highly desirable for its own sake, but it is also something which candidates will be expected to demonstrate in the examination. It is important to note that to understand a particular teaching, practice etc. is not the same as merely to have an opinion concerning it. Understanding may be accurate or inaccurate, perfect or imperfect, true or false. Moreover, to understand is not in itself the same as to believe or to approve of. One may have an accurate understanding of any teaching or practice, even if one does not believe it or consider it valuable. One purpose of questioning and discussion therefore is to ensure that pupils really do *understand* what a doctrine means (or does not mean), what a particular practice signifies or is meant to signify etc., irrespective of subjective attitudes. It is concerned with meaning.

Distinct from this are questions which are asking pupils to *evaluate*—to give or assess opinions (their own or others') on the relevance, implications, validity, utility etc. of some teaching, practice, argument, attitude etc. In the examination, answers to such questions will be assessed on the quality of argumentation, the capacity of a candidate to identify issues/possible implications etc, and to marshal relevant evidence/arguments for and/or against particular views. It is important therefore for pupils to have the experience of engaging in discussion of this kind, i.e. in *evaluation* discussion. Some questions and activities aimed at promoting such discussion are included in the Student Text and in this Guide.

Teachers may well, however, wish to supplement these with other examples.

In most Units, the Student Text contains SUMMARIES at periodic intervals. These are intended to help pupils consolidate their grasp of key points and to provide an aid for revision.

Content of the Teacher's Guide

Not all the material in the Student Text is equally important. Some is vital; some is more peripheral, or included simply for added interest. The notes on the Units try to give guidance to teachers on the key points to be stressed and the main features to be emphasised. In addition to explanatory comments on some of the exercises/activities, 'model' answers are generally given to sets of questions appearing in the Student text. It is hoped that these will be found useful for quick reference.

On occasion, extended *background notes* of a theological nature are given. Though these may include elements which may be presented to at least some pupils, it must be emphasised that their primary purpose is not to provide material for specific lessons, but to help teachers themselves to see topics in a wider context, to help them in providing additional explanations which may be needed or in dealing with questions which may arise. They are intended as aids to assist the teacher's own understanding, so that he/she may avoid false or unhelpful emphases, and may approach the enterprise with more confidence and discernment.

A wide range of methods and teaching styles may be employed in the delivery of this syllabus, and the Teacher's Guide makes no attempt to be prescriptive. In both the Student Text and the Guide there are suggested activities which include, for example, suggestions for dramatisation, role play, and work of a graphic or pictorial character (individual or group). These are included only as suggestions, and are not meant to be comprehensive or exhaustive. It is, however, considered advisable for teachers to employ a range of activities, in order to maintain variety and interest and also to cater for the various needs of individuals and groups.

In particular, the employment of drama techniques should not be despised. Certain scenes and topics from Scripture lend themselves very well to treatment in this way, and the use of drama/role-play can be very useful in helping pupils to identify and appreciate the various factors/viewpoints/constraints/influences operative in a variety of life situations. Such techniques, however, though very useful, are not self-sufficient. Issues and attitudes, once identified, need to be discussed, analysed and evaluated.

In general, it may be said that activities involving pictorial work (posters, displays, collages etc.) may be found most useful as a summative exercise, at the end of some topic or section of a topic. Drama/role-play may be found more useful as a preliminary stimulus exercise or at least as an intermediate stage in the treatment of some topic or issue.

Teachers will be aware of many resources, teaching aids and sources of information which are available. A few are indicated at various points in this Guide, but the list is very selective and could easily be supplemented. One very important resource for assisting the teacher's own knowledge and understanding of Catholic teaching is the *Catechism of the Catholic Church* (Chapman 1994). In the notes on some of the Units, lists are given of articles from this Catechism relevant to particular areas or issues. These lists indicate only some of the most important articles, and are not meant to be comprehensive. It is hoped, however, that they may provide a source of initial easy reference. In some Units, a list of other relevant Church documents is given, which may be found useful as background reading for teachers.

'Q Source'

One resource which may be found useful, and which deserves special mention, is a computer software package called 'Q Source'. It provides information from a variety of sources on matters relevant to the syllabus. It is being continually expanded and updated. Further information concerning it may be obtained from: Q-Source Software, 9 The Town Green, Mill Street, Kidlington, Oxford, OX5 2EJ.

UNIT 1

JESUS CHRIST

Section A : Who Is Jesus?

This Section deals successively with the topics detailed in the syllabus content, and includes treatment of the texts prescribed in connection with these, as appropriate. In the outline given below, indication is given of the subsection(s) in which texts *prescribed in the syllabus* occur. Other texts referred to or quoted in the Student Text, either for the purpose of illustration or further elucidation or for the sake of added interest, do not receive specific mention.

Outline of Section A

1. *Introduction—Who does he think he is?*
   Actions of Jesus which provoke questions.
   Texts: *Mt 8:23–27; Mk 2:1–12.*

2. *Jesus is The Christ*
   Peter's answer at Caesarea Philippi
   Exercise on John The Baptist; notes on Peter and Elijah.
   The meaning of 'Christ'
   Summary
   Texts: *Mk 8:27–30* (and *1:1–20*)

3. *Son of the Father*
   Jesus's use of the word 'Father'
   Jesus and his Father according to St John
   What is meant by calling Jesus 'Son of God'
   Texts: *Jn 17:1–6, 14:6–10*

4. *Word of the Father*
   Use of words: to express one's self—to get things done
   The power of God's Word
   Jesus as the perfect expression of God
   Texts: *Jn 1:1–18*

5. *Jesus—the Lord*
   Use of God's Holy Name
   Jesus Christ is Lord
   My Lord and my God
   Summary
   Texts: *Jn 8:51–59; Phil 2:6–11; Jn 20:24–29*

6. *Three Persons—One God*
    Mystery
    The Mystery of the Trinity (in brief)

7. *Other Professions of Faith*
    The Letter to The Hebrews
    The Creed
    Summary
    Texts: *Heb 1:1–3*, relevant portion of the Creed

8. *Born of the Virgin Mary*
    The role of Mary in God's plan
    The meaning of the virginal conception of Jesus
    Texts: *Lk 1:26–39*

1. Who Does He Think He Is?   [pp.3–5]

Many people who are not Christians would think of Jesus as: a
good man, a 'religious genius', a great moral teacher, etc. Muslims
consider him to be a great prophet. Christians go much further than
this.

The testimony of the New Testament concerning Jesus is conveyed
not just through explicit assertions concerning him, but also
through the implications of his words and actions. Questions were
first of all raised in people's minds before answers were arrived at.
The aims of this subsection are:

* to help pupils to understand that the actions and words of Jesus
  provoked questions about who he was, and suggested certain
  answers;
* to encourage them to ask similar questions.

2. Jesus is the Christ   [pp.6–8]

Introductory Note
The identification of Jesus as 'The Christ' underlines the continuity of the New Testament with the Old. Jesus is the fulfilment of
God's plan and his promises. At the same time, however, he
exceeds expectations. He comes to bring a greater 'peace', a
greater liberation and a greater Kingdom than the people of Israel
commonly expected, and he was himself someone greater than
even they imagined. The aim of this subsection is to help pupils
understand the significance of calling Jesus 'the Christ'.

[p.6]   In order to answer the questions concerning *Mk 1:1–20,*
pupils may be referred to a Bible, or they may be supplied with a
copy of the text as given overleaf.

Mark 1:1–20

The beginning of the Gospel of Jesus Christ, the Son of God.
As it is written in Isaiah the prophet,

> Behold, I send my messenger before thy face,
> who shall prepare thy way,
> the voice of one crying in the wilderness;
> Prepare the way of the Lord,
> make his paths straight—'

John the baptizer appeared in the wilderness, preaching a baptism of repentance for the forgiveness of sins. And there went out to him all the country of Judea, and all the people of Jerusalem; and they were baptized by him in the river Jordan, confessing their sins. Now John was clothed with camel's hair, and had a leather girdle around his waist, and ate locusts and wild honey. And he preached, saying, 'After me comes he who is mightier than I, the thong of whose sandals I am not worthy to stoop down and untie. I have baptized you with water; but he will baptize you with the Holy Spirit.'

In those days Jesus came from Nazareth of Galilee and was baptized by John in the Jordan. And when he came up out of the water, immediately he saw the heavens opened and the Spirit descending upon him like a dove; and a voice from heaven, 'Thou art my beloved Son; with thee I am well pleased.'

The Spirit immediately drove him out into the wilderness. And he was in the wilderness forty days, tempted by Satan; and he was with the wild beasts; and the angels ministered to him.

Now after John was arrested, Jesus came into Galilee, preaching the Gospel of God, and saying, 'The time is fulfilled, and the kingdom of God is at hand; repent and believe in the Gospel.'

And passing along by the Sea of Galilee, he saw Simon and Andrew the brother of Simon casting a net in the sea; for they were fishermen. And Jesus said to them, 'Follow me and I will make you become fishers of men.' And immediately they left their nets and followed him. And going along a little further, he saw James the son of Zebedee and John his brother, who were in their boat mending the nets. And immediately he called them; and they left their father Zebedee in the boat with the hired servants, and followed him.

Questions [p.6]

1. The message of John the Baptist and the initial message of Jesus were similar—'Repent!' John was preaching in the wilderness, and Jesus spent some time at the beginning of his ministry in the wilderness.

2. Yes. Not only does he not contradict Peter, but he charges the Apostles 'to tell no-one about him'—which suggests that he accepted the truth of what Peter had said.

The fuller account of this scene in Matthew is dealt with in Unit 4: The Church.

Elijah and the Prophets

The Old Testament references are not prescribed texts, but may be found interesting. The account of Elijah being 'taken up' led to the expectation that he would return some day. In addition, there was a prophecy of the return of Elijah in Malachi 4:5.

The Christ [p.7]

Again, the Old Testament references are not prescribed texts, but they may be useful in encouraging pupils to investigate the idea of 'Messiah'. The kind of Kingdom is described in general terms in the 3rd text (Is 9:1, 5–7). Other messianic texts are Is 11:1–5, Jer 23:5–6, Ezek 127:22–24. For the purposes of the examination, pupils need only a general idea of the messianic expectation.

Key Points

The meaning of 'Christ'
The Jewish expectation that the Christ will establish God's Kingdom.

The Belief of The Church [p.8]

The Preface of Advent is not a prescribed text. It is merely illustrative.

Something to Do (Extension Exercises) [p.8]

1.   An opportunity for research into contemporary Jewish understanding of the Messiah.

2.   This is intended to promote further consideration of the relationship between beliefs about Jesus and attitudes to his message. To serve as a good basis for discussion, a wide variety of views should be collected, both positive and otherwise.

3. Son of the Father [pp.9–11]

Background Note

God as Father — In the Hebrew Old Testament, God is occasionally (on eleven occasions) referred to as 'Father' of Israel, but is not directly addressed as 'Father'. Jesus, however, goes far beyond such an occasional idea of God as 'Father' in a general sense. When speaking of God, he is shown as *routinely* referring to him as 'the Father' or 'my Father', and also speaks of himself as 'Son'. For Jesus, moreover, 'Father or 'my Father' is not merely his *typical* mode of address to God (which would itself be wholly exceptional) but in fact the *only* mode of address which he employs. In the Gospels, the person of Jesus is defined by his relationship to God as 'Son' to his 'Father', and God himself is presented as, above all, the 'Father' of Jesus.

Abba — We are specifically told that Jesus used this aramaic word 'abba' for 'Father', when addressing God. 'Abba' is not, as is sometimes said, a childish diminutive (equivalent to 'daddy'), but it was the normal everyday word used by both children and adults for addressing their fathers. The fact that Jesus uses this word, rather than the formal Hebrew of the synagogue, helps to underline the intimacy of the relationship which is being asserted. There does not appear to be any example of the use of 'abba' as an address for God before Jesus.

St Paul's express mention of the term tends to support the idea that this usage of Jesus was quite distinctive. It is significant that, when St Paul wishes to express the intimacy of the relationship with God which union with Jesus brings, he speaks of Christians specifically crying out 'Abba, Father'. The fact that he does this not only in the Letter to the Romans (written mainly to Jewish Christians) but also in the Letter to the Galatians (written mainly to Gentiles) strongly suggests that he is not merely using a term which is part of his readers' everyday speech, but one which is specifically recommended by the usage of the Lord.

Texts — Of the references on p.9, only Mk 14:33–36 is prescribed. It reads as follows:

> And he took with him Peter and James and John, and began to be greatly distressed and troubled. And he said to them, 'My soul is very sorrowful, even to death; remain here and watch. 'And going a little further, he fell on the ground and prayed that, if it were possible, the hour might pass from him. And he said, 'Abba, Father, all things are possible to thee; remove this cup from me; yet not what I will, but what thou wilt.'

Verse 36 is the key passage here, because of the use of 'Abba'. For the purpose of this unit, the rest is only included to put it in context.

Both the texts from John on p.10 are prescribed.

The aims of this subsection are:
- to introduce students to the intimacy of the Father–Son relationship between Jesus and God, conveyed by the New Testament.
- to promote understanding of the traditional teaching about Jesus as 'Son of God'.

The key ideas, which are introduced here, and developed in subsequent subsections are:
- that Jesus is the eternal Son of God, who is from the very being of God, and who has always existed;
- that, because of this, even in his humanity, he is the one who is a perfect reflection in human terms of what God is like, of what his attitudes and concerns are, so that to know Jesus is to know God, to see him is to see the Father.

The two passages from John on p.10 give indications along these lines: the first particularly with regard to Jesus's pre-existence, the second in respect of Jesus as the one in whom God becomes visible.

The remaining material in the subsection is concerned with an explanation of the Father–Son analogy, which, like all analogies based on human realities, is not perfect.

With regard to this explanation, it is important to stress, from the start, that according to Christian teaching the eternal Son, who became man in Jesus Christ, is in himself eternal and *uncreated*. Though he takes on a created humanity, he is not in himself one of God's works, but eternally from the very being of God. This point is elaborated in subsequent subsections.

4.   *Word of the Father*   [pp.12–15]

This subsection centres on the Prologue of the Gospel of John. It complements and further explores the ideas introduced in subsection 3. It is important, first of all, to discuss the importance of human words. The key ideas are that words are:

- means through which we express ourselves;
- means through which we get things done;
- not merely external things which we use, but things which come directly from us, which belong to us, are part of us.

These ideas are then applied to the analogy of Jesus as the one perfect Word of the Father.

[p.12]   Introduction to the nature and function of human words.

[p.13]   The passage from Matthew is not a prescribed text, but is used as an example to illustrate the power of words, and as an introduction to consideration of the special power of God's Word.

Questions
The centurion is a person in authority. His words produce effects because of that authority, which causes others to obey him. He has behind him the authority of military discipline, and ultimately the power of the Roman Empire. Jesus's words also have authority,

but an authority which not merely causes others to obey, but which can directly bring things about. Jesus's words, like God's, have power in themselves.

[p.14]   In the Scriptures, there are numerous instances where God 'speaks'—to reveal his will, his purposes, and to bring them about. Jesus is not merely one way in which God 'speaks'. He is *The Word* through whom God perfectly expresses himself, and through whom he brings about all his purposes. It is important to stress, from the beginning, these two aspects:

- The Word who *reveals:*
- The Word who produces effects.

[p.15]   The point being made is that the Son is eternally 'The Word', in whom the Father expresses himself to himself, and through whom he creates. At a point in time this eternal Word takes on a human nature, and 'The Word became flesh'. He then becomes the personal self-expression of God *for us*, in terms we can understand.

Questions
This examination of the prescribed text (Jn 1:1–18) is the key element of this subsection. Questions and answers will need to be thoroughly discussed. Here are some 'model' answers:

1.   The connection is suggested by the opening words 'In the beginning', and confirmed by the following 'all things were made through him', and without him was not anything that was made'.

2.   He was in the beginning with God'.

3.   Some are:
'... and the Word was God' (explicit);
'All things were made through him' (attributing to him the divine work of creation);
'In him was life' (since life comes from God).
There is, however, much room for discussion on the implication of other expressions.

4.   'All things were made through him etc.'

5. Because he existed before him (and yet John was born before Jesus).

6. 'Power to become children of God'

7. The eternal Word became a human being, was born into the human race, and shared our life. (N.B. The literal meaning of the phase translated 'and dwelt among us' is 'and pitched his tent among us' i.e. chose to become part of our human society).

8. In both cases they express the idea that he 'comes forth' from God's very being—as a child from his father, and as a word comes from the mind and the mouth of the one who speaks it.

9. 'The only Son (i.e. Jesus) has made him known.'

10. The first part requires a personal response. Among attitudes it reveals are: a desire to be united with us, an attitude of care and concern. It should give believers confidence in God's concern for human beings and in his desire to form a personal relationship with them. It should encourage the idea of God as someone who is not remote, but very close, and committed to humanity.

5. *Jesus — the Lord*   [p.16–20]

The principal aim of this subsection is to explore the meaning and implications of calling Jesus 'the Lord'. Closely connected with this is the application to Jesus of God's Holy Name. The key points are:

• that to call Jesus 'the Lord' is to apply to him a divine title, which is in fact a substitute regularly used for YHWH, the Holy Name of God, which no Jew would dare to pronounce, but which in the New Testament is actually used of Jesus himself;

• that to call Jesus 'the Lord' is therefore to identify him as divine, entitled to the worship due to God alone;

• that when Christians call Jesus 'the Lord' or 'my Lord' or 'our Lord' they are expressing also that he is the one to whom they owe their complete loyalty.

[p.16] The outline of the account of the revelation of God's name in Exodus is only meant as general background information. The key point is the Name itself: I AM.

[p.17] The prescribed text (Jn 8:51–59) is the classic obvious example where Jesus is shown using God's Name as his own. 'Before Abraham was, I AM' (not 'I was'). The reaction of the Jews as described by John, seems to indicate that the implications were not lost on the audience. Stoning was the penalty for blasphemy.

In order to understand the implications of the two references in Question 5 (which are not prescribed texts), it is necessary to realise that the Greek for 'I am he' (*'Ego eimi'*) literally means simply 'I am'. There seems in both cases to be at least a play on words, with a double meaning. See also the accounts of Jesus walking on the water in both Matthew (14:27) and John (6:20), where Jesus's words, translated as 'It is I', are in Greek, once again, simply *'Ego eimi'*.

YHWH   [p.18]
This material is included mainly for added interest. Pupils may be expected to know that YHWH are the letters of the Holy Name, but will not be expected to know how to write or recognise it in Hebrew. An important point, however, is the extreme reverence for the Name shown by Jews, and hence the use of the term 'Lord' as a substitute for it. To call someone 'The Lord' in the fullest sense therefore was equivalent to calling him divine.

Jesus Christ is Lord
This prescribed text from Philippians is very important, and needs thorough discussion. It emphasizes both the reality of Jesus's adoption of the human condition, as one of us, even to the point of accepting death, but also his divinity—one who was divine from the beginning, and who is entitled to the Name and worship due to God alone.

Questions (first set)   [p.19]

1. Becoming a man.

2. Accepting death on a cross.

3. From 'emptying himself...' to '... even death on a cross'.

4. There is only one such name: the Name of God—YHWH.

5. Everybody should give him divine worship. '... at the name
    of Jesus every knee should bow, in heaven and on earth and
    under the earth.'

6. The passage from Isaiah reads: 'To me every knee shall bow,
    every tongue shall swear.' The worship therefore which this
    passage from St Paul considers due to Jesus is the worship
    which in Isaiah is due to God.

My Lord and My God
In a sense, the whole of St John's Gospel leads up to this dramatic
profession of faith. It is the summary of the Christian's view of
who Jesus is, in the light of the Resurrection.

Questions (second set)

1. An Apostle.

2. The marks of Crucifixion in his hands and side; the fact that
    people could touch him.

3. He appeared among them, although the doors were shut.

4. It is obviously because he believes that Christ's victory over
    death confirms his claims and establishes his divine status.

5. In the Prologue: 'and the Word was God'.

6. The words are addressed to all Christians throughout the ages.

Something To Do   [p.20]
In addition, or as an alternative to the suggested dramatization
(which could include the previous scene when Thomas was
absent), pupils could be asked to write Thomas's own account of
these events, and of how he felt.

Additional Activity
Discuss the following in groups or as a class:

• If Christians believe that Jesus is their 'Lord', what kind of
  attitudes should they have towards him?

• What kind of effect should that have on the way they live? Why?

Then make a poster or display illustrating your conclusions, with the title:

JESUS THE LORD

6. Three Persons — One God   [pp.21–22]

The principal aim is to encourage an appreciation, in outline, of the meaning and importance of the general doctrine of the Blessed Trinity, as required by the syllabus. This is something which is in any case necessary at this point. We have talked of Jesus as God, Son of God etc., and also of the Father as God. And yet there is only one God. Some treatment of the Trinity is necessary, in order to make the doctrine concerning the divinity of Jesus intelligible.

Mystery
There is a preliminary treatment of the concept of 'mystery'. This and the subsequent material on the Trinity may pose particular difficulty, and should be carefully discussed with the class. There is a useful and amusingly illustrated treatment of 'mystery' in *How to Survive Being Married to a Catholic* (Redemptorist Publications) pp. 4–5, which may be found helpful. The aim here is to draw attention to the fundamental difficulty involved in talking about a Being so immeasurably superior to us. The key sentence in the Student's Text is: 'Only God can fully understand God.'

We can learn a number of things about God, but he still remains in himself an unfathomable mystery. We can say *what he is not*, but when we want to say *what he is*, we have to use analogies taken from the created world, saying in effect, 'God is something like this.' Because God is not part of created reality, all such analogies can only be imperfect, but since these analogies (or images) come to us through the revelation God has made of himself in the Scriptures, and especially in Jesus Christ, we can be confident that, with the guidance of the Holy Spirit, they can enable us to say and believe true things about him, even though in only a limited way, and even though we will never fully comprehend the depths of that truth.

A possible objection is that one cannot believe in something one does not understand. But this simply does not follow. We all quite happily, and quite reasonably, believe in the existence of a force called gravity, and yet, as it happens, no-one fully understands gravity. The world is in fact full of things we do not, and possibly never will understand, but which we know to be true.

Discuss with the class (non-religious) examples of 'mysteries', things you can never completely get to the bottom of. Find examples of questions whose answers give rise to new questions, and so on ad infinitum.

The Mystery of the Trinity   [p.22]
The fundamental Christian mystery, but not the only one, is the mystery of the Trinity. There is an old story about St Augustine of Hippo, who wrote one of the great theological treatises on the Trinity. One day he was walking on the sea shore and saw a small boy on the beach, picking up one grain of sand at a time. When he asked what he was doing, the boy replied that he was trying to count the exact number of grains of sand on the shore. 'What a foolish idea', said Augustine, 'to suppose that you could ever do that'. 'Not so foolish', said the boy, 'as to suppose that you could ever fully understand the Trinity.'

Bearing the above rebuke in mind, the following, which is an expanded version of what is in the Student Text, seeks to clarify the theological picture.

The early Christians believed that there was only one God, but that not only the 'Father' but Jesus himself and also the Holy Spirit were divine. They had to find a way of trying to make clear what they meant and did not mean by saying this. To do this, they employed the concepts of 'person' and 'nature'.

Our human nature is the sum of all our attributes: our body, spirit, intelligence, will, capacities etc. Because we are all human beings, our natures are fundamentally similar, and for this reason we can talk of a common 'human nature' which all share. We are all the same kind of being, all members of the same species, and therefore all connected and related to each other. This is important because it means that when the Son of God becomes man, he enters into a relationship with human nature as a whole, with the whole human race and every member in it.

Nevertheless, within this unity of the human race, each human being remains an individual being. Each of us has his/her own individual human nature. Each of us is also a *person*. This is something difficult to define. Perhaps the best that can be said briefly is that it is what we refer to when we use the word 'I'. Each of us is an 'I', a personal subject, who possesses a human nature, and relates to other persons, other 'I's, in a way different from the way we relate to non-personal creatures. The distinction between nature and person can be illustrated by asking the questions 'What?' and 'Who?' The answer to 'What am I?' is 'a human being'. The answer to 'Who am I?' is my name. Our nature is what we 'possess' and operate through. Our person is the one who possesses and operates.

Christians believe that there is only one God, one divine Being, one divine nature, but that in that one God there are three Persons. This is difficult for us to grasp, because each human person is an individual human being with his/her own individual human nature. There are therefore as many individual human natures as there are human persons. We find it very difficult to imagine one divine nature 'possessed', so to speak, by three distinct Persons, three 'I's, whom we call Father, Son and Holy Spirit.

Although we find it difficult, the idea does provide us with a way of understanding, at least to some extent, how it can be true to say that there is only one God, and also that both Jesus and the one he called his Father are truly God. The idea is that each of the divine Persons possesses the fullness of the one identical divine nature—that is to say, everything that belongs to God, and that moreover they are united together in love to an extent beyond our comprehension. They act with a common will, intelligence and power. All are eternal and inseparable. None existed before the other. All are equally the one true God. When we have said all this, we are still dealing with something we can never fully understand, but we do have some idea of the reality we are talking about.

When we call one Person Father and another Son, we are using human language to try to convey some idea of the relationship between them. It cannot do this perfectly, because here we are applying human terms to the infinite and eternal God, who is very different from human beings. They are, however, the words which God has given us to describe this relationship, and therefore Christians are sure that they do point to a true resemblance, however limited that may be. To speak of a Father/Son relationship in God is not to imply that God's Fatherhood is precisely the same as that found among human beings. It does point, however, to a relationship whereby one Person eternally comes forth from the other, and eternally receives from him the fullness of the divine nature. It also points to a relationship in which the two are united by a bond of love similar to that between a good father and a good son, but infinitely greater.

The mystery of the Trinity is impossible to understand fully, but it is not something which has been revealed simply to mystify us. It not merely gives us an insight, however limited, into the relationship between Jesus and his Father, but it tells us something of immense importance about God in himself. The one God, in the Christian understanding, is not a solitary being who needs to create, in order to have something or someone to love other than himself. God is in himself a relationship of love—love between Persons. He is not a solitary 'I', but a Being with an inner personal life, who invites us through his Son, Jesus Christ, to share with him that inner life and love of his. The greatest law Jesus gave us is the law of love. That is because God himself *is* love, and we are called to be like him and to be united with him.

7.   *Other Professions of Faith*   [p.23–24]

This subsection, especially the part concerned with the Nicene Creed, seeks to bring together most of what has been dealt with so far.

The Letter to the Hebrews

1.   'All things were made through him' (Prologue);
      'through whom also he created the world' (Hebrews).

2.   '... and bears the very stamp of his nature'.

3. '... through whom also he created the world' and
'... upholding the universe by his word of power'
(attributing to Jesus the creation and sustaining of the
universe).

Questions on the Nicene Creed [p.24]

* '... became incarnate'—'was made flesh' (Prologue)

* Light represents goodness and is a symbol of God. God the
Father is light and also the source of light. The light which
comes from him is as truly light as the light which he is. We
may think of the Father as the 'unapproachable light' (cf.
Eucharistic Prayer 4) which dazzles us, and the Son as the
light of day, which comes from him, and by which we may
see. The idea is given in Heb 1:3, where Jesus is called 'the
radiant light of God's glory'.

* Through him all things were made.'
In Prologue: 'All things were made through him'.
In Hebrews: '... through whom also he created the world'.

Notice how the Creed employs the themes already found in the
Scriptures.

8. *Born of the Virgin Mary* [pp. 25–26]

The aim of this subsection is to explore the role and importance of
the Blessed Virgin Mary in the Incarnation, as required by the
syllabus. There are two key points:

• As the mother of Jesus, Mary's role is vital. It is from her, by
the power of the Spirit, that Jesus becomes one of us. Her
motherhood is the guarantee of Jesus's true humanity.

• She performed her role freely, in faith and obedience to God,
and so is rightly honoured as the great example of faith for
Christians.

The title of 'Mother of God' is very ancient. It was confirmed by
the Council of Ephesus in 431. It does not, of course, mean that
Jesus derives his divinity from Mary. What it does mean is that the

child whom Mary bore was not merely a human child, but also the eternal Son of God.

The Annunciation passage from Luke, which is a prescribed text, is fairly straightforward.

Questions

1. The fact that she was specially approached; the words 'Hail, O favoured one, the Lord is with you'.

2. 'The Holy Spirit will come upon you and the Power of the Most High will overshadow you'.

3. The words indicate that Mary considers herself God's servant, and that she consents to his plan for her.

The 'Virgin Birth' [p.26]
(See also the Creed [p.23]).

> 'For us men and for our salvation he came down from heaven; *by the power of the Holy Spirit* he became incarnate *from the Virgin Mary* and was made man'.

It is important to go carefully over the notes on the virginal conception. The doctrine of the 'Virgin birth' is not merely a 'biological' assertion, though it is that; it is a doctrine with important messages concerning who Jesus is and what his mission is.

The Immaculate Conception
The doctrine of the Immaculate Conception is not part of the syllabus. The note concerning it on page 26 is included partly as additional information, but partly to distinguish this doctrine from the 'virgin birth' or 'virginal conception' of Jesus, with which it is often confused. Sometimes it is even erroneously thought that it is a doctrine which asserts that Mary herself was virginally conceived!

Catechism of the Catholic Church

The following are some of the articles from the Catechism which may be found useful in regard to the topics dealt with in this Section.

The Christ (436–440); Son/Word of God (240–242, 443–445, 461–464, 479–483); The Lord (446–451); The Trinity (237, 249–256, 260–267); Born of The Virgin Mary (484–5, 495–497, 502–511).

Section B : The Mission of Jesus

This Section deals with the topics dealt with in the syllabus content, and includes treatment of the texts prescribed in connection with these, as appropriate. As in Section A, in the outline given below, indication is given only of where *texts prescribed in the syllabus* occur.

Outline of Section B

1. *Introduction—Jesus at Nazareth*
   Texts: Lk 4:16–22

2. *Revealing God's Love*
   Love and Union—The Crucifixion
   The Story of Fr Damien in relation to the mission of Jesus

3. *Victory over Death—One meaning of Jesus's Resurrection*
   SUMMARY
   Texts: Jn 3:16; 1 Cor 15:12–20; 1st Preface of Christian
   Death; Committal Prayer: 'In sure and certain hope...'

4. *Achieving Salvation*
   Dying for someone—St Maximilian Kolbe
   Dying for our sins—Jesus The Saviour
   Sacrifice of Atonement—Yom Kippur—Priest and Victim
   Ransom/Redemption
   The value of Jesus's death
   Texts: Rom 5:6; 1 Cor 15:3; Mt 26:28; Heb 9: 11–12;
   10:11–14; Mk 10:45; Eph 1:7; Col 1:13–14; 1 Pet 1:18–20

5. *The Triumph of The Resurrection—Liberation from sin*
   Relation of the Crucifixion to the Resurrection
   SUMMARY

6. *Was it necessary for Jesus to suffer and die?*
   SUMMARY
   Texts: Jn 3:16–17; Rom 5:6–8; 1 Jn 4:9–11; Heb 4:14–16;
   Portions of the Creed

7. *Communicating Salvation*
   Stories illustrating acceptance of salvation

A new beginning
The Holy Spirit
Accepting Salvation—A living faith
SUMMARY
Texts: Rom 5:19; 1 Cor 15:22; Mt 16:24; Jn 15:12–14;
Portions of the Creed

8. *The Life of the World to Come*
Judgment, Heaven, Hell, Purgatory
Final Exercise
Texts: Portions of the Creed

1. Introduction [pp. 27–28]

The aim of this subsection is to start pupils thinking about some of
the main themes involved in a consideration of Jesus's
mission—especially the idea of liberation. The starting point is the
declaration Jesus himself makes at Nazareth, using the words of
Isaiah—and which is a prescribed text. It is a description of the
mission of the Christ (Messiah). The reference to 'anointing',
explained in the notes on p.28, makes this clear. Jesus claims that
the prophecy refers to him ('Today this Scripture has been fulfilled
in your hearing'). This description of his mission therefore follows
from his position as 'The Christ'.

Questions [p.28]
After going through the text with pupils, it is probably better if the
teacher allows them to engage in free discussion on the questions,
and come up with their own provisional answers. It is to be
expected that, as they progress through this Section, they will
develop further ideas and insights. The teacher may help by
drawing attention to certain ideas but at this stage it is probably
best not to attempt to secure fully-rounded and informed answers.
It may be that pupils are left with more questions than answers, but
at this stage this is not a bad thing. These questions will be
readdressed at the end of the Section, to see what new insights
pupils have gained.

It would be useful, however, for teachers to underline the key idea
of 'liberation', when it occurs, especially in regard to questions 2

and 3, and notions such as 'faith' and 'truth' in regard to question 4.

The ability of pupils to answer question 5 will depend on previous knowledge. Examples may be concerned with those oppressed by illness, poverty, guilt etc. They may be examples of Jesus's own actions or of concerns expressed in parables or other items of teaching. If pupils find difficulty in recalling examples, teachers should supply some for them to discuss.

Activity
This is based on the note on 'the acceptable year of the Lord' in the body of the Student Text (p. 28). Its aim is to reinforce the idea of Jesus's mission as one of 'liberation' from 'slavery', and to encourage reflection on the meaning and experience of 'liberation' in someone's life.

Preliminary Remarks to Subsections 2 and 3

Subsections 2 and 3 (pp.29–34) form a unity. The complete union (solidarity) with us which Jesus achieves through sharing our death is mirrored in the hope of our union with him in his Resurrection. Together these two subsections consider the Crucifixion and Resurrection as the way in which Jesus shares our death in order to overcome it for us, but they begin (in subsection 2) with the foundational consideration of the life and death of Christ as the great expression of God's love for mankind.

2. Revealing God's Love   [pp.29–31]

The aim is to develop understanding of the idea of Jesus's willingness to share our lot, and particularly our death, as the supreme expression of the depth of God's love. It follows on naturally from previous material in Section A on Jesus as the 'Word' of God.

Love and Union
The ideas raised here are fundamental, and should be carefully explored. They form the basis for the rest.

Father Damien   [p.30]

The syllabus does not require knowledge of this account or any
details of Damien's career. It is included here as a concrete
example of love shown by someone completely identifying
himself with others. It is simply meant as a way of illustrating
the kind of 'solidarity' with mankind shown by Jesus. Fr
Damien was *beatified* in 1994.

Questions

2.   The question is meant to draw out this connection.

3.   This gives opportunity for mentioning other examples.
     Mother Teresa might be mentioned, but there are many
     other possibilities.

The underlying point is that by sharing our lot, Jesus clearly shows
God's concern for us and his wish to be united with us, and this is
clearly shown *most fully* in Jesus's willingness to accept suffering
and death. God's love is ready to accept all that being united with
us involves. These considerations, which are explained on p.31,
should be thoroughly discussed with pupils.

3. Victory Over Death   [pp.32–34]

The aim is to develop understanding of the Resurrection as the
foundation of the Christian hope of eternal life. This subsection
completes the previous material. Jesus not only shares death with
us, but overcomes it for us. The illustration on p.33 shows the risen
Christ drawing others up with him. The title in Greek is
Anastasis— which means 'Resurrection'. subsections 2 and 3
together explore one aspect of 'salvation'. Jesus unites himself
wholly with us through his Crucifixion, and so his victory over
death becomes our victory also.

The prescribed passage from 1 Corinthians is a classical text on
the Resurrection. It will be further considered in subsection 5.

Questions
These are mainly designed to draw out the connection between the
Resurrection and the Christian hope of life after death.

1. Belief in the Resurrection of Christ necessarily involves belief in the Resurrection of the dead.

2. Because being a Christian is not easy: it was (and is) likely to involve sacrifice and possibly persecution. In St Paul's time especially it was dangerous to be a Christian. If this life was all that was on offer, it was rather a grim prospect for them.

3. The 'first-fruits' represent the whole harvest. To say that Christ is the 'first fruits of all who have fallen asleep' (i.e. the dead) is to imply that the risen Christ typifies what is offered to all who have died. In other words, Paul is telling Christians that the fact that Christ is risen means that they also will rise with him to new life.

The First Preface of Christian Death   [p.33]
This is a prescribed text, which should be first read with the class. Pupils could then be asked for their initial reactions to it. Is it morbid, joyful, pessimistic, optimistic etc? What kind of attitude to death does it encourage? The teacher should initiate discussion (or otherwise draw attention to) those parts which particularly reflect the beliefs already dealt with, e.g. the fourth stanza (beginning: 'In him who rose from the dead....').

Questions
These are mainly designed to encourage reflection on the implications of belief in the Resurrection for people's attitudes and behaviour. Answers will be personal, but the following observations include some points worth considering.

1. Encourage pupils to discuss why and in what way. A positive answer might mention the comfort that hope in a future life can supply.

2. Probably. A positive answer might mention fear of suffering, of extinction, of the unknown, of possible future judgment etc.

3. It depends. They might, for example, fear judgment for misdeeds.

4. Possible answers might include: confidence in God's mercy and goodness, a good conscience, consciousness of repentance for misdeeds.

5.   A number of possibilities, depending to some extent on beliefs concerning the connection between this life and the life to come. It should help people to concentrate on what is really valuable and lasting.

In Sure and Certain Hope   [p.34]
The committal prayer is also a prescribed text. The most significant feature, and the one which supplies the answer to the subsequent question on this page, is the content of the opening two lines: 'In sure and certain hope of the resurrection to eternal life through our Lord Jesus Christ.' This prayer is used at the moment of burial. The last part of it is the 'Aaronic blessing', i.e. the blessing modelled on that used by the priest, Aaron in the Old Testament (cf. Num 6:22–24).

Something to Do
This is an extension exercise. The aim is to deepen understanding of Christian attitudes to death. The main Catholic observance is the Funeral Mass, followed (usually) by the committal—either by burial (which is the traditional and still the preferred option) or cremation (which is nowadays permitted). Often the body is brought into church the evening before the funeral. Then, after a short service, it is left in the church overnight. There is also the practice (particularly common in certain countries, including Ireland) of relatives and friends praying around the body at the home of the deceased. Consideration could also be given to the general practice of prayers, Masses for the dead, memorial cards asking prayers for the dead, observance of All Souls' Day etc. (These are also mentioned in Unit 4—The Church—page 203). Liturgical details may be found in the Catholic Rite of Funerals. Pupils might also consider aspects of the Anglican (or some other Christian) funeral rite. If this exercise is undertaken, however, it is better to concentrate on one or two items and seek to understand them well, rather than simply gather a mass of assorted pieces of information.

Alternative Activity
Pupils might make a poster/display on the Resurrection, entitled:

VICTORY OVER DEATH

Preliminary Remarks to Subsections 4 and 5

Just as subsections 2 and 3 go together, so do 4 and 5. Where 2 and 3 explore the Crucifixion and Resurrection of Jesus in regard to the overcoming of death, 4 and 5 widen the perspective to include the overcoming of sin.

Background Theological Note

Salvation in its perfected form is union with God. Jesus's work of salvation is the means by which he makes this possible for human beings. This is what he achieves through his life, death and Resurrection, and is sometimes called the 'objective redemption'. The basic idea is that, though salvation comes as a gift from God, this gift was *earned* by Jesus's self-offering on the cross, an offering of love which more than makes up for human sinfulness. It is in and through his humanity that Jesus, the Son of God, offers his sacrifice, and therefore the will of God to save us is brought about through one of us. The human race therefore is saved not simply from 'outside' (by divine decree) but from within—through Jesus Christ. Through his death and Resurrection Jesus restores the harmony between God and his creation, destroyed by sin, and establishes in himself a new kind of human existence and a new relationship with God which human beings are now invited to share. For this to become a reality for individuals, however, it needs to be communicated and accepted. Such acceptance, brought about by the work of the Spirit, is each person's 'subjective redemption'. Its other technical name is 'justification' (see the marginal note on p.45).

Subsection 4 deals only with the 'objective redemption' achieved by Jesus. The communication and acceptance of that redemption (justification) is dealt with in a later subsection.

4. Achieving Salvation   [pp.35–39]

The principal aim is to promote understanding of the death of Jesus as the means of overcoming sin, by which human beings are alienated from God. In connection with this, it deals with the notions of atonement, ransom/redemption, reconciliation.

Key Concepts
The text deals with various ways of looking at Jesus's work of salvation, particularly the idea of his death as a sacrifice of atonement and as a work of ransom/redemption. Underlying both of these, however, are two basic concepts which are relatively easy to communicate.

- the idea of someone acting in place of/on behalf of others;
- the idea of 'making up' or 'making amends' for something.

Any pupil who can understand the basic meaning of these two relatively straightforward concepts can understand the main thrust of this part of the Unit.

St Maximilian Kolbe
The syllabus itself does not require any knowledge of Maximilian Kolbe. This account is used as an illustrative example of the concept of self-sacrifice—giving one's life for others, to save others—acting/suffering *in place of* others, for their benefit. Its purpose is to provide a basis for the further consideration of the sacrifice of Jesus.

Questions

1. He gave up his life for the sake of the other, who was able to live because of Maximilian's action.

2. For personal judgment by pupils.

3. (As above).

4. Many examples from the lives of the saints/martyrs, or various heroic deeds. Everyday examples could include reference to classes of people who risk/sacrifice their lives for the common good or to save others, e.g. firefighters, rescue teams, bomb disposal squads etc.

Dying For Our Sins
It is advisable for the teacher first to go over each of the quotations (all of them prescribed texts) with the class.

Questions   [p.36]

1. God's love (Rom 5:8).

2. '... for the forgiveness of sins' (Mt 26:28).

Jesus The Saviour

This material provides the connection with the story of St Maximilian, and the basis for what follows. It should be discussed carefully. Note particularly:

- the *full* meaning of 'eternal life' in the first paragraph;
- the idea of sin as separation from God, which needs to be cancelled out;
- the distinction between the limited 'salvation' effected by St Maximilian, and the perfect salvation achieved by Jesus.

[p.37]   One way of looking at the salvation Jesus achieves is to think of it as a *sacrifice of atonement*, by which, out of love and obedience to his Father, and from love of humanity, Jesus offers himself totally, to 'make up for', 'make amends for' all human refusal of love and obedience to God. This is the vision of the author of the Letter to the Hebrews, who models his account on the ritual performed by the High Priest on Yom Kippur. Jesus is the true High Priest, who represents the whole of humanity. The sacrifice he offers is not the blood of animals, but himself—a sacrifice so valuable in God's eyes that it can truly 'make up' for all human sinfulness in a way nothing else could. The key sentence is: 'His offering is an offering of himself in love, to make up (atone) for all humanity's lack of love.'

The two quotations from Hebrews [pp.37–38] are both prescribed texts.

Questions   [p.38]

These are designed mainly to bring out the significance of the similarities and contrasts between the sacrifice of Jesus and other sacrifices. Students may need considerable help in dealing with the questions.

1(a) Heaven.

  (b) Presenting his sacrifice before God the Father in heaven. 'Blood' here is a symbol for the self-sacrifice of his death on the Cross, when he shed his blood.

2.   They are inferior to Jesus's sacrifice, because they are incapable of taking sins away. They have to be *performed* time and time again, but Jesus offers one perfect sacrifice.

(The question of the Eucharist as a participation in the offering of this one sacrifice will be dealt with in Unit 4, pp. 223–4.)

3.   Numerous possible examples.

4.   The answer is obvious, but it will be interesting to obtain reasons from pupils. One reason is that any action of ours in itself can only have a limited value. The case is different with Jesus, because of who he is.

5.   The answer to the first part is in the marginal note on page 37.

A Work of Redemption [p.38]
This is an alternative way of stating a similar idea. Here Christ's death is thought of as the price which he pays to set us free. It is the 'cost' which he incurs, in order to bring about our liberation. Again, there is the same basic idea. Only something as valuable as the self-offering of Christ can 'make up' for sin (or pay off the 'debt'). Only that can actually 'earn' for us salvation. It may be advisable to discuss first of all various examples of 'redemption', as indicated by the text.

Questions (first set) [p.39]

1.   Through his death on the Cross.

2.   Slavery of sin—since redemption is considered as 'forgiveness of our trespasses' (Eph. 1:7) and 'the forgiveness of sins' (Col. 1:14)

The Value of Jesus's Death
Both ways of looking at salvation depend upon Jesus's death having a particular value. The two questions in this portion of the text, together with the quotation from 1 Peter (and possibly Phil. 2:6–11), are meant to promote ideas on why this should be so. Fundamentally it is because Jesus, though truly a man, is also the eternal Son of God, and therefore this total offering of himself is infinitely valuable in God's eyes. It is an absolutely pure self-offering. Jesus himself was without sin; he deserved no punishment. His sacrifice was one he had no need to make; it was not at all for his benefit, but for the benefit of others. There was no trace of self-interest. It was a sacrifice of pure love and obedience.

Because God is love, all acts of truly unselfish love are valuable in his eyes, but Jesus's supreme act of love stands in a class apart because of who he is. To get the idea across, pupils should be helped to appreciate how astonishing is the idea that someone who was the eternal Son of God, through whom all things were made, should be prepared to suffer and die in agony for our sake, though he had no need to, and though he had done nothing to deserve it. There could be no greater demonstration of love and humility.

Because he is God's beloved Son, Jesus's sacrifice has infinite value. Because he has also truly become man, he can make the offering in his humanity, as our representative—enduring human suffering and death, and offering it for our sake with a human will, and with human as well as divine love.

Guarantee of the Certainty of Forgiveness

The teacher may like to develop with pupils the idea that, because Jesus's sacrifice is so valuable in God's eyes, Christians can be utterly sure that God will never refuse forgiveness to anyone who repents, no matter how great the sin or *how impossible adequate reparation on our part may seem*. The basic Christian assertion is that reparation for all sins has already been made by Jesus Christ. He has done what we cannot do. All we have to do is accept *through faith and repentance* the reconciliation he has won for us. This is one of the central messages of the Crucifixion, and that message may be considered as one of the reasons why the Crucifixion formed part of God's plan of salvation.

Activities [pp.38–39]

Two possible extension activities on the theme of 'Redemption' (one pictorial, one written) are suggested in the margin of page 38. In addition, an activity based on the 'suffering servant' passage in Isaiah is suggested in the margin of page 39. This is most suitable for more able pupils. This text from Isaiah is not a prescribed one, but it may be useful in helping some pupils to deepen understanding of the idea of 'vicarious suffering' (i.e. suffering in the place of, and on behalf of, others) in relation to the sacrifice of Christ.

5. *The Triumph of the Resurrection* [p.40]

This subsection complements the material in subsection 4. Its principal aim is to clarify the connection of the Resurrection with the redemptive sacrifice of Christ.

In subsections 2 and 3 the basic idea was that in his Crucifixion Christ shared death with us, and in his Resurrection he overcame it for us. In 4 and 5 the basic idea is that in his Crucifixion Christ took upon himself, and atoned for, sin and its consequences, and in his Resurrection he offers us the reconciliation and new life with God he has won for us. The Resurrection therefore reveals and establishes:

- Christ's triumph over death;
- Christ's triumph over sin (separation from God).

In both cases it is a triumph Christ won *for us*. The new life of the Resurrection is a life in which sin and death have been overcome. It is a share in that life which Christ now offers. The Resurrection of Christ is seen as Christ's *vindication*. It is the sign:

- that he is who he said he was;
- that his sacrifice has been accepted;
- that therefore salvation and eternal life with God are ours, if we want them.

That is why it is so fundamental to Christian faith. If there had been no Resurrection the death of Christ would appear meaningless.

Questions

1. It makes clear that Jesus's death was a victory, not a defeat; that his self-offering has been accepted by God the Father; that his death marked not the end of Jesus and his message, but the entry into a new kind of human existence, which is offered to all.

2. It would probably have died with Jesus.

The excerpt from the Preface of Palm Sunday is not a prescribed text. It is merely illustrative of the faith and teaching of the Church.

Activity

Pupils might be asked (individually or in groups) to summarize this topic by drawing a series of pictures/symbols, accompanied by a written explanation.

6. *Was it Necessary for Jesus to Suffer and Die?* [pp.41–42]

The aim of this subsection is to help pupils appreciate reasons why the Crucifixion of Jesus is considered a particularly appropriate means of bringing about salvation. One reason is initially given on p.41, and there is then a brief summary of additional reasons on p.42. These will need to be further explored and explained. Consideration of the four Scriptural texts (all prescribed) should help in doing this. The following points may be found helpful:

(1)   It is the willingness of Jesus to die for our sake that proves to us in the clearest possible way how much God loves us. (cf. the first three texts, from John, Romans and 1 John). This both enables us to have the greatest confidence in God and his mercy, and is a powerful motive for us to return that love.

(2)   In particular, the fact that Christ died for us 'while we were yet sinners' (Rom. 5:8) assures us that all sins have been taken into account. Christ died for them all, and therefore all can be forgiven. One might add that in Luke's Gospel Jesus is shown as praying for his executioners. This is an additional demonstration that no sin, even putting to death the Son of God, is beyond forgiveness.

(3)   [cf. the 4th text, from Hebrews] The fact that the Son of God himself, who intercedes for us with his Father, is also one of us, that he has been through all we have to go through, including temptation, suffering and death, and the fact that he has done it all for our sake, gives us a sure basis for confidence in his understanding of our difficulties, in his compassion and assistance.

(4)   Evil and disharmony have come into creation through human sinfulness. It is right that humanity should be involved in the overcoming of evil and the restoration of harmony. It is through Christ's humanity that this is achieved, and that

'expiation' is made for our sins (cf. 1 Jn 4:10). Because he is truly man, redemption comes to us not just from 'outside'—from the love and mercy of God—but also from 'within'. In this way God shows his respect for human dignity.

(5) In suffering and dying for the rest of the human race, Christ gives us an example and pattern of how we must conduct ourselves, if we want to share in the salvation he has won for us. [This point will be developed in a subsequent subsection].

This is how the ideas in (4) are expressed in the 3rd Preface for Sundays:

> We see your infinite power
> in your loving plan of salvation.
> You came to our rescue by your power as God,
> but you wanted us to be saved by one like us.
> Man refused your friendship,
> but man himself was to restore it
> through Jesus Christ our Lord.

Other points relevant to this question will be dealt with in subsequent parts of this Unit.

The Creed   [p.42]
This material serves as a epilogue to all of the Unit so far. The Creed summarizes the main points of Christian belief in the salvific nature of Christ's mission:

• that the Son of God became man 'for us and for our salvation';
• that he was crucified 'for our sake'.

It is only because of the actual historical life, death and Resurrection of Jesus that Christians believe in salvation and eternal life. The Creed therefore is careful to underline the *factuality* of what it asserts. This is a very important point. The Christian Church never thought of these things as merely a kind of fable with an encouraging message. They believed that salvation and forgiveness and an eternal destiny had been offered to human beings precisely and only because the Son of God had actually become one of us, had actually atoned for our sins by his death, and had actually risen from the dead to offer us eternal life with God.

The SUMMARY is particularly important, and should be given careful attention.

7. *Communicating Salvation* [pp.43–46]

Previous material has dealt with what Jesus has achieved for humanity. This part is concerned with how the salvation he has achieved is communicated, how individuals can share in the Resurrection and new life he has won for them. This subsection is very important. It reflects the basic Catholic belief that, though it is Jesus (and not we ourselves) who has won salvation, and though that salvation comes to us as a free gift which we do not deserve, and have not earned, nevertheless we have a part to play. God gives us the grace to accept the offer of salvation, but we can still refuse. Moreover, acceptance involves not only belief and trust in Christ, but also a life lived in love, expressed in good deeds. The principal aims of this subsection are to help pupils to understand the teaching that:

- while Jesus has won salvation for all, it is a gift which human beings can reject;
- acceptance of salvation involves not just faith and trust, but also the attempt to live a life of love—doing good and avoiding wrongdoing, in imitation of Jesus;
- the reconciliation and new life won for human beings by Jesus is communicated through the gift of the Holy Spirit.

Two Stories
The two stories are easy enough to understand. They are meant to illustrate what is meant by acceptance of salvation. Note that salvation here is equated with liberation—freedom. The second story particularly makes the point that some kinds of 'slavery' can seem quite congenial, and that true freedom may bring its own difficulties, and require courage and effort. This is a theme teachers may like to explore and develop.

Question 2

This is concerned with the parable of the Sower (not a prescribed text for this Unit). It may be found useful as an additional (and Scriptural) stimulus for discussion on this matter.

A New Beginning [p.44]

This is a further extension of the same idea, but it focuses specifically on Christ as 'new start' for the human race, the beginning of a 'new creation'. People have a choice. Do they want to belong to the inheritance of the 'first Adam', which is an inheritance of sin (separation from God) and death, or to the inheritance of the 'last Adam', which is one of union with God as his children, and eternal life with him? This part restates the idea of Christ as 'Leader'—which raises the question of what following his leadership involves.

Questions

1. The relationship of being reconciled to God; the relationship of children of God, sharing Jesus's own relationship with his Father.

2. By leading the kind of life Jesus lived and taught; by prayer, worship, participation in the Eucharist; by obeying Jesus's teachings. (Pupils should be encouraged to give specific examples of what that would involve).

The Holy Spirit [p.45]

It is important to emphasize the role of the Holy Spirit. The Spirit is considered to be the personal bond of love between the Father and the Son. It is through the gift of the Spirit that sin (separation from God) is taken away, and we are reconciled and united with God. It is through the gift of the Spirit that we are given a share in Jesus's relationship with the Father—as adopted children of God. Salvation is therefore trinitarian. It comes to us from the Father, through the saving work of the Son (Jesus), by the power of the Holy Spirit. The gift of the Spirit *is* each person's salvation, but it is a gift which can be rejected or only imperfectly accepted.

Questions

1. Because it is through him that we receive the gift of a share in God's life (grace) as his children.

2.   (Actually 2 statements)
'... who proceeds from the Father and the Son' (i.e. comes
forth from their very being;
'With the Father and the Son he is worshipped and glorified'.
Only someone who is God can be entitled to the same
worship as the Father and the Son. Calling the Holy Spirit
'the Lord' also implies this.

Accepting Salvation—A Living Faith
This material concentrates on the Catholic teaching that mere
belief is not sufficient for true acceptance of the salvation offered
by Christ. What is needed is faith made alive by love and
expressed in good deeds, in accordance with Christ's teaching. The
point should be made that the love in question is itself a gift of
God's grace. Any act of 'living faith' is only possible with the help
of God. No-one can live as a Christian simply by his/her own
efforts. The help of God's grace is always needed, but it can be
refused. The three Scriptural passages (including one on page
46—all prescribed) provide a basis for discussion of what is
involved in the 'living faith' a true disciple of Christ should have.

Grace and Justification
The marginal notes may be found useful for explaining common
terms which are often very imperfectly understood. 'Justification'
is merely the technical term for the communication/acceptance of
salvation. For examination purposes, it is not really necessary for
students to know it, but since it occurs frequently in St Paul, it is
useful for them to know what it means.

Questions   [p.46]

1.   He/she should follow the example and teaching of Jesus, and
this will not always be easy. Examples: 'Let him deny
himself, and take up his cross and follow me', 'love one
another as I have loved you'—Jesus's love led him to the
Cross. 'When he was reviled, he did not revile in return etc.'

2.   Numerous possibilities.

3.   Being prepared to suffer hardships for Jesus's sake, or the
sake of others, or in the cause of right.

4.   Rejecting sin, and living according to God's will.

5.	In his Crucifixion Jesus took upon himself the consequences of our sins, and atoned for them.

6.	Jesus's suffering and death is the 'medicine' which cures our sinfulness.

7.	A dead faith is a faith which is merely belief, not expressed in the way we live our lives. A living faith is faith lived out in love, expressed in good deeds.

Activities
Each of the suggested activities is aimed at consolidating and developing pupils' understanding of what the Christian life involves.

## 8.	*The Life of the World to Come*	[pp.47–48]

This part is very straightforward. The material in it is sufficient to meet the requirements of the syllabus. Its aim is to promote an outline understanding of the terms Judgment, Heaven, Hell and Purgatory. The proper emphasis is:

- *Heaven* (eternal life with God) is what is intended for us by God.
- *Hell* (eternal separation from God) is what we can choose. We choose it by separating ourselves from God through grave sin of which we refuse to repent. This is in effect a refusal of grace, a refusal of salvation.
- Those who have not separated themselves from God in such a way, but still are imperfect, are not denied Heaven. They need, however, purification from their faults, if they are to live with God, who is perfect love and goodness. *Purgatory* is a doctrine based upon the mercy and compassion of God.

The Creed
All that is needed is a very basic outline understanding of the meaning of the various assertions in the Creed. The Ascension, as such, is not part of the syllabus. It is sufficient for pupils to understand this as meaning that Jesus is now 'with God'.

'Seated at the right hand of the Father' means that Jesus, even in his humanity, now enjoys divine honour and glory. The presence of Jesus at God's 'right hand' marks the inauguration of the Messianic Kingdom.

'From thence he will come....' It is sufficient to know that this is the coming of Christ at the end of time, to conduct the final general judgment.

'Resurrection of the dead'. This refers to the belief that, just as Jesus rose in his full humanity ('body and soul'), so the dead generally will rise in their full humanity, but a humanity transformed, freed from the limitations of earthly life. Useful references are: Phil. 3:21; 1 Cor. 15:42–44,53.

Questions

1. It could cause people to take more seriously questions about how they ought to behave. It could help them to try to live good lives. On the other hand, it might cause some to live lives full of fear and anxiety. The teacher might care to discuss the latter point, if it arises. If a Christian is living an evil life, he/she has good cause to fear. But for a Christian who is honestly trying to follow Christ, even if he/she fails from time to time, the antidote to such fear and anxiety is trust in God's goodness and mercy and assistance, and a constant readiness to repent.

Final Exercise

(a) is meant as a revision exercise, and as a means of identifying remaining points of confusion.

(b) gives an opportunity to pupils to answer again the questions on Jesus's description of his mission in the synagogue at Nazareth, incorporating now any additional insights they may have gained.

Catechism of the Catholic Church

The following are some of the articles from the Catechism which may be found useful in regard to topics dealt with in this Section.

Revealing God and his love (65–66, 458–459, 515–516); Achieving Salvation (456–7, 599–623); Resurrection (651–655, 988–991); Justification, Grace etc. (1708, 1815–1816, 1987–2002); the Life of the World to Come (1021–1041).

UNIT 2

THE PASSION AND RESURRECTION
OF JESUS

This Unit deals with the account of the Passion, Death and Resurrection of Jesus according to Luke, and also with the celebration of key events in that account in the Liturgy of Holy Week. Each of these elements of the Unit, the Scriptural and the liturgical, are in fact examined in different papers in the examination, and it would be possible to deal with each sequentially, for example by studying the Scriptural narrative as a whole first of all, and then dealing with all the liturgical topics. It was, however, considered more advantageous to approach matters in the manner employed in the Student Text, i.e. by dealing successively with a portion of the Gospel text followed in each case by the liturgical celebration related to it. It is hoped that this will provide greater interest and variety, as well as helping pupils to appreciate in a more direct fashion the relation of the liturgical celebration to the biblical account and the events it records.

Teachers may, however, choose to reject this method, if they so wish, and may prefer to deal with section (a) and (b) of this Unit sequentially, as they are laid out in the syllabus content. If they do so, however, they should note that the syllabus requires that candidates 'be able to relate relevant elements of the narrative to the liturgical features detailed in section (b)' and *vice versa*. In other words, these two parts of the Unit must be taught in a way which relates each to the other. That consideration alone supplies a good reason for adopting the approach which is actually followed in the text.

At the beginning of the Unit (p.50) is an OUTLINE OF MASS. This is intended as a general reference aid. In this Unit it may help pupils to see where special liturgical elements, mentioned in connection with particular feasts, fit into the general structure of the total celebration. Reference is made to it at various points in the Student Text. It may also be useful in respect of some of the material in other Units, especially Unit 4.

Outline of Unit 2

Introduction
> St. Luke's Account: the Characters
> Holy Week

1. *From the Entry to the Passover*
   The Messiah enters Jerusalem (19:29–40,41–44)
   Palm Sunday   -   How the Church celebrates
                  -    in Israel
   After the Entry: Opposition Grows (19:47–20:47)
   SUMMARY OF EVENTS

2. *Maundy Thursday*
   Conspiracy and preparation (22:1–65)
   The Origins of the Passover Meal
   The Institution of the Eucharist (22:14–20)
   Other Sayings of Jesus (22:21–38)
   The Mount of Olives (22:39–46)
   Maundy Thursday: How the Church Celebrates
   The Arrest of Jesus and Peter's Denial (22: 47–65)
   SUMMARY OF EVENTS

3. *Good Friday*
   Jesus on Trial (22:66–23:25)
   Summary of the situation
   The Way to Calvary and the Crucifixion (23:26–48)
   The Burial of Jesus (23:50–56)
   SUMMARY OF EVENTS
   Commemoration of Good Friday

4. *Easter*
   The Empty Tomb (24:1–12)
   The Road to Emmaus (24:13–35)
   Jesus appears to the Apostles—The Ascension (24:36–53)
   Evidence for the Resurrection
   Easter—How The Church Celebrates
   The Easter Vigil
   Easter Sunday
   (The Celebration of Easter in the Byzantine Rite)

Introduction [p.51]

This includes general introductory material on both the Lucan account and on Holy Week. Further general information on Luke and his Gospel may be found at the beginning of Unit 3 (Alternative A) on pp.93–94. The syllabus requires some knowledge of the general characteristics of Holy Week. Information on this point is given on p.53.

Teachers should note carefully the requirements detailed in the syllabus content in respect of knowledge, understanding etc. that pupils should have in regard to the Lucan narrative. The treatment in the Student Text is designed to meet these requirements. The summaries which are included at regular intervals should help to ensure a knowledge of the sequence of the main events, and may be found useful as revision aids.

1. From the Entry to the Passover [pp.54–60]

19:29–40
Questions

1. Palms. [This is explained in the first paragraph on p.56.]

2. King.

3. Joyful, e.g. 'the whole multitude of the disciples began to rejoice'.

Question [top of p.55]
They help us to understand that Jesus is being presented as 'the Christ', and therefore why this event was considered important. It is the entry of the Messiah who comes to establish God's Kingdom.

Questions

1. His compassion, and his care and concern for the people of Israel.

2. That it would be short-lived, that it was superficial.

3. It has an air of foreboding. It suggests that events will change for the worse.

Palm Sunday — How The Church Celebrates [p.56]
Whatever the deficiencies in the attitude of those who welcomed
Jesus into Jerusalem, the Church now, in its celebration of Palm
Sunday, acclaims Jesus as the true Messiah (the Christ), in full
knowledge of who he really is and of the salvation he has come to
secure.

On Palm Sunday, the Church welcomes and acclaims the
beginning of the final and decisive phase of Christ's saving work,
the beginning of the events that lead to his suffering, death and
Resurrection. There is therefore a mixture of joyful acclamation of
the one who comes to achieve salvation and sorrow because of the
prospect of the suffering he had to endure.

In the opening rites, including the blessing of palms and the
procession, the emphasis is on rejoicing, but the later dramatic
reading of the Passion underlines what the events of Palm Sunday
are leading to. The reading of the Passion on this day puts the entry
of Jesus into context. It presents it as not just an isolated event, but
as the beginning of a drama which will be progressively unfolded
during Holy Week.

Questions [p.57]
1. Initially mainly joyful, but a more sombre mood is also
    indicated, especially through the reading of the Passion.

2. Year 3 (or C).

3. The traditional hymn is 'All glory, laud and honour'.
    Another is 'Ride on, ride on in majesty'. The latter captures
    very well the mixture of rejoicing and sadness appropriate to
    this celebration.

In Israel [p.58]
This part is merely added for the sake of interest. It is not
information which candidates will be expected to have for
examination purposes.

Aids and Activities
The best aid would be the attentive presence of pupils at the
celebration of Palm Sunday. The same is true in respect of the
other liturgical celebrations dealt with in this Unit. In school,

Christ, Church & Life : Teacher's Guide

pupils could be shown examples of the kind of palm leaves received by members of the congregation (and also of the 'palm crosses' into which these are traditionally made). Sometimes churches are decorated with whole palm fronds (which may also sometimes be carried by clergy and others in the procession). Where possible, examples of these may be brought into school. It may be possible to obtain old ones from a local parish church, or alternatively it may be possible to purchase some from an ecclesiastical supplier (e.g. Hayes and Finch) during Lent.

The full liturgy, including readings, may be found in any Catholic Sunday Missal. Pamphlets containing all the main Holy Week services (Holy Week 'missalettes') are also published relatively cheaply by a number of firms. (These include the Catholic Printing Co. of Farnworth, and Goodliffe Neale & Co.) It might be useful to have a few copies of these available.

A reading of the Passion, in the way prescribed for Palm Sunday, could be staged in class. If well done, this can be very effective. The Lectionary or a Sunday Missal will show how the narrative is apportioned to the various readers. If this is to work properly, the pupils chosen must be good at reading aloud, and should be thoroughly rehearsed beforehand.

For videos, see the notes at the end of this Unit.

After The Entry — Opposition Grows [pp.59–60]

The above title indicates one of the important themes in 19:47–20:47. It has already been foreshadowed in the question on p.55 on the reaction of Jewish leaders to Jesus's 'cleansing of the Temple'.

19:47–20:8
Questions

1. John the Baptist.

2. Probably because he knew that they were only seeking some way to destroy him. They would probably have accused him of blasphemy or sedition and tried to have him arrested. Jesus counters the attempt by showing up their hypocrisy.

20:9–19 (Parable of the wicked husbandmen)
Questions

1. He is warning them that, by failing to live as God wishes, by persecuting his servants, and plotting to kill Jesus himself, they are risking rejection by God, who will entrust others with his Kingdom. Jesus is here foretelling his own execution.

2. It represents all that God has bestowed on his chosen people, the people of Israel.

3. Jesus.

4. It represents them as enemies of God and indicates that others will be entrusted with God's gifts, such as the covenant and the promises. That is why they say, 'God forbid!'

20: 20–40 (Tribute to Caesar etc.)
Questions

1. If Jesus said it *was* lawful to pay these taxes, he would be accused of supporting Roman rule, which the Jews hated. If he said it was *not* lawful, he would be accused of inciting rebellion against Roman rule.

2. Every Jew knew that *everything* belonged to God, and that he owed him his entire allegiance. Jesus is separating the idea of paying taxes from the idea of giving allegiance. He is saying, in effect, 'It is the Emperor's coinage, so let him have it, but be sure to reserve your whole loyalty to God'. In this way, he avoided inciting a rebellion, while at the same time avoiding support for Roman rule.

3. Life in the world now is different from life in the world to come. There will be no need of marriage there. Therefore the Sadducees' question is pointless. In the rest of the passage Jesus is simply pointing out that, if Abraham, Isaac and Jacob had simply been annihilated, never to live again, God could not properly be called their God any more. To think otherwise was to think of God as the God of the dead—and this Jesus rejects.

4. Because the scribes were almost exclusively Pharisees, who believed in resurrection. The Scribes were delighted that Jesus had so effectively answered the Sadducees and had agreed with their position on this matter.

The *Exercise* (p.60) is designed to consolidate pupils' understanding of this aspect of the 'plot' of the Passion narrative, and also to act as a revision exercise. It may be done orally or in writing, individually or in groups.

2. *Maundy Thursday* [pp.61–68]

22:1–65 (Conspiracy and Preparation)

Questions

1. The Feast of Unleavened Bread.

2. Without yeast: unleavened bread does not rise.

3. They feared that the people would become Jesus's followers.

4. Judas Iscariot: he plotted with the chief priests to betray Jesus.

The Origins of the Passover Meal
This is included as background information. For examination purposes, pupils do not need to know all this detail. The essential points are that the Passover was the celebration by the Jews of their liberation from slavery in Egypt, and their establishment as God's chosen people.

The Structure of the Passover Meal
In dealing with this matter with pupils, the outline overleaf may be found useful.

The Seder (in the time of Jesus)

PRELIMINARIES
(The participants would be reclining on couches)

- Words of dedication were said over the First Cup of Wine (The 'sanctifying cup')

- A preliminary course of herbs was served.

- The *Haggadah* — This gave an explanation of the meaning of the celebration. In a family setting (which was the normal setting for the Passover) the youngest son would ask the father a number of set questions: on why this day was different from other days, and on the meaning of the various items of food etc. The father gave answers which brought out the meaning and significance of what was being done. For example, the unleavened bread was 'the bread of affliction' and the bitter herbs which formed part of the meal represented the bitterness of the slavery they had to endure. Reference was also made to the lamb and other features of the celebration.

- Then the first part of the 'Hallel' Psalms (Psalms 113–114) was sung.

- After this was the Second Cup of Wine (the 'cup of rejoicing').

THE MEAL PROPER

- Blessing over *unleavened bread* which was then broken and distributed to all.

- Meal of roasted lamb, bitter herbs etc.

- *Thanksgiving* over *the third Cup of Wine* (the 'cup of blessing'), from which everyone drank. (Though the ritual involved four cups of wine, it was only obligatory for everyone to drink from this third cup).

CONCLUSION

- The second part of the 'Hallel' Psalms (Psalms 115–118) was sung.

- Words of praise over the fourth Cup of Wine (the 'cup of redemption').

Note that the emphasis is on the bread and wine at the beginning and end of the meal proper. It is to these elements that Jesus gives a new meaning. In the Christian Eucharist, the rest disappear. In particular, the central feature of the Jewish celebration, the Passover lamb, no longer features in the Christian Eucharist. It is replaced by the new 'Lamb' whose sacrifice takes away the sins of the world—Jesus Christ himself.

The Eucharist   [pp.62–63]
The meaning of the Eucharist is treated in greater detail in Unit 4, especially pp.223–5 and 231–2. Here the key points are:

- Jesus identifies the bread as his Body and the wine as his Blood.

- He clearly makes a connection between what he is doing here and the death he is about to undergo.

- He shows that he is establishing a new ritual which he wants his disciples to continue, by saying, 'Do this in remembrance of me.'

Questions   [p.63]

1. They have in common that they all admit a connection between the Eucharist and the sacrifice of Christ on the Cross. The main difference is that the Catholic view sees the Eucharist as a real participation by the Church in the offering of Christ's sacrifice, and asserts that what is received in Holy Communion is Jesus Christ himself, really and substantially present in the Sacrament. Other views see the Eucharist as something merely symbolic, which calls to mind the sacrifice of Christ and helps to strengthen faith in him. (This is something of a generalisation, since there is a broad spectrum of non-Catholic views. It does, however, represent a relatively typical and 'classical' protestant attitude. Further notes may be found in the material on Unit 4.)

2. Those who hold the Catholic view are more likely to emphasize the importance of the Eucharist and to see it as central to Christian life, and because they believe that Jesus Christ is truly present in the Sacrament, they are likely to treat it with great reverence. For similar reasons they are likely to attach great importance to its institution by Jesus on Maundy Thursday.

22:21–38 (Other sayings of Jesus at the Last Supper)
Questions   [p.64]

1. Unlike what happens generally in the world, those among
    Jesus's disciples who have authority must act in a spirit of
    service, in imitation of Jesus himself.

2. By performing his functions in a spirit of service to others,
    for their benefit and not his own, putting their interests before
    his own.

3. '... and when you have turned again, strengthen your
    brethren.'

4. (a) 'but behold, the hand of him who betrays me is with me
        on the table' (v.21).
    (b) Only that it will be serious. 'Woe to that man by whom
        he is betrayed'.
    (c) It is someone who is with him at the table.
    (d) Judas Iscariot.

5. What he does, he does not for his own benefit, but for that of
    others.

22:39–46 (The Mount of Olives)
Questions   [p.65]

1. That he was distressed at the thought of the suffering that
    awaited him, but that nevertheless he wanted above all to do
    his Father's will. That was the most important thing for him.
    [This is a useful question to discuss further. Jesus is shown as
    fully human. He no more relishes the thought of an agonizing
    death than anyone else. In fact, he shrinks from the prospect
    of it. Jesus is perfectly obedient to the will of his Father, but
    that does not mean it is easy for him.]

2. The suffering in store for him.

3. It is a sign of the intensity of his supplication.

4. Among some that might be suggested are:
    Real courage consists in the overcoming of fear, not its
    absence.
    The most important thing is to live the way God wants us to,
    no matter what the cost.

It may sometimes be necessary to suffer, in order to do what we should, but Christians are not expected to like it. There is nothing wrong with wanting to be delivered from it, as long as we are prepared to do God's will in any case.

Jesus Christ really does know what pain and fear and suffering are like. So Christians can be confident that he sympathises with them, and that he will help them.

Maundy Thursday—How the Church Celebrates   [pp.66–67]

The addition to the Eucharistic Prayer, mentioned on p.67, occurs in Eucharistic Prayer 1 (the Roman Canon). There is also a special form of the section of this Prayer beginning 'In union with the whole Church' and 'Father, accept this offering'. These go as follows (additions in italics):

> In union with the whole Church
> *we celebrate that day*
> *when Jesus Christ, our Lord*
> *was betrayed for us....*
>
> Father, accept this offering
> from your whole family
> *in memory of the day when Jesus Christ, our Lord,*
> *gave the mysteries of his body and blood*
> *for his disciples to celebrate....*

In the Missal, there is an instruction that the homily at the Mass of the Lord's Supper should explain the principal mysteries which are commemorated. These are specified as:

- the institution of the Eucharist;
- the institution of the priesthood (because Christ tells the Apostles 'Do this in remembrance of me');
- Christ's commandment of brotherly love.

'Watching' before the Blessed Sacrament   [p.67]
The inspiration for this practice comes, of course, from the episode of Christ's prayer in Gethsemane (the 'Agony in the Garden'). In Luke's account the disciples are told, 'Pray that you may not enter into temptation' (22:40) and 'Rise and pray that you may not enter into temptation' (22.46), when Jesus returns to find them asleep. It

is, however, the accounts in Matthew and Mark which have particularly encouraged the practice. Here Jesus tells the disciples to 'watch and pray', and then, when he returns to find them asleep, asks 'Could you not watch one hour with me?' (cf. Mat 26:38–41; Mk 14:34–38). It is this question especially which Catholics have addressed to themselves. They therefore spend some time in prayer with Jesus on this evening which commemorates his prayer in the Garden and his arrest.

Readings on Maundy Thursday
The Gospel reading at the Mass of the Lord's Supper is John's account of Jesus washing the disciples' feet. The institution of the Eucharist is commemorated in the Liturgy of the Word by the Second Reading, which is St Paul's account of the institution in 1 Corinthians.

Aids
The text of the Liturgy and the Readings for the Mass of the Lord's Supper and for the principal liturgies of the rest of the 'Easter Triduum' (Solemn Liturgy on Good Friday and the Easter Vigil) will be found in most Sunday Missals, intended for the congregation. Alternatively the Liturgy may be found in The Roman Missal and the Readings in the Lectionary. For videos, see the notes at the end of this Unit.

22:47–65 (Arrest of Jesus and Peter's Denial) [p.68]
Questions

1.   Judas had told them.

2.   Probably because he was too popular among the people.

3.   There were few people about, and no fear of a popular disturbance.

4.   Darkness = evil. This is when the power of evil has its way.

5.   Probably panic at the thought that he too might be arrested.

6.   We are told (23:62): 'And he went out and wept bitterly', when he remembered that Jesus had foretold that he would deny him.

7.   At the Last Supper.

3. *Good Friday*

Jesus on Trial

It is important for pupils to understand the reasons for the two trials (p.69) and Summary (p.70).

The notes concerned with the danger of anti-semitism [p.69] are also very important. They reflect the strong statement made to this effect by the Second Vatican Council (Vatican II *Nostra Aetate* 4, in A. Flannery, Vatican Council II, Vol. 1, pp.740– 742). The main substance of this is also repeated in the Catechism of The Catholic Church 597–598, which includes a quotation from an earlier 'Roman Catechism' (the Catechism of The Council of Trent) which forcefully puts the blame for Christ's death where it fundamentally belongs.

> Since our crimes made our Lord Jesus Christ suffer the torment of the cross, those who plunge themselves into disorders and evil unquestionably crucify the Son of God anew in their hearts, for he is in them, and hold him up to contempt by their sins. And we must acknowledge that our crime in this case is greater than that of the Jews. As for them, according to the witness of the Apostle, 'None of the rulers of this age understood this; for if they had, they would not have crucified the Lord of glory.' We, however, profess to know him. And when we deny him by our acts, we in some way lay our murderous hands on him.

The Catechism of The Catholic Church also quotes St. Francis: 'Nor did demons crucify him; you have crucified him and crucify him again, by delighting in your vices and sins.'

22:66–23:25

69 'Son of Man' has the characteristics of the divine figure mentioned in Daniel 7:13–14, to whom 'was given dominion and glory and kingdom, that all peoples, nations and languages should serve him.'

70 'You say that I am' (*ego eimi* in Greek)'. It seems likely that 'I am' here is a reference to the divine Name.

1. Forbidding tribute to Caesar and claiming to be a King (23:2).

2. Whether it was lawful to pay tribute to Caesar. Jesus had replied: 'Render to Caesar the things that are Caesar's, and to God the things that are God's.' (cf. 20:21–25).

3. He probably hoped that Herod would deal with the matter in some way, and so relieve him of a difficult decision.

4. See at least 23:4,14,15,20,22.

5. Individual judgment. Some might think he was weak and cowardly, perhaps well-meaning but lacking the courage of his convictions.

6. They had to have a political rather than a religious charge. For the Roman authorities to act, there had to be a charge which constituted an offence against Rome. It also had to be a charge which the Romans would punish with death.

23: 26–48 (The Way to Calvary and the Crucifixion)
Questions [p.73]

1. Because a Christian is supposed to imitate Christ in being ready to endure anything in order to do God's will.

2. (a) Obvious.
   (b) that he will receive acceptance from God; that he has obtained salvation.
   (c) Anyone who turns to Jesus, no matter how bad he/she has been, and no matter how late in life, can receive forgiveness and salvation.
   (d) He acknowledged that he had done wrong, and that he deserved punishment. He implicitly expressed faith in Jesus, even in these circumstances, and appealed to his mercy. He was honest about himself. He was not vindictive. Though he was a sinner, he believed in God. He had respect for goodness and could recognize it, when he saw it. There are plenty of other plausible answers.

4. See 23:29,34,43.

5. It is an expression of sorrow and/or shame.

29:50–56 (The Burial of Jesus)
Question   [p.75]
Because it is these women who will find the tomb empty.

Things to do   [p.74]
A basic purpose of both these activities is to consolidate pupils'
knowledge and understanding of the Passion narrative, and of the
various attitudes to Jesus. The first encourages pupils to enter
imaginatively into the situation, and to develop awareness of its
meaning for and affect on those who were involved.

Psalm 22 is the one beginning: 'My God, my God, why have you
forsaken me ?' This task is more literary and investigative. One
aim is to develop pupils' understanding of the Christian view of
Jesus as the one in whom God's plan of salvation is fulfilled. He is
the one who fulfils the Scriptures. This task is probably more
suitable for the more able pupils.

Commemoration of Good Friday   [pp.76–78]

The Entry   [p.76]
This act of prostration is very rare in Catholic liturgy. It is a
dramatic expression of humility, repentance and adoration before
God. The principal other instance when it occurs is during the
singing of the litany in the ritual for the ordination of deacons,
priests and bishops. Then the candidate for ordination also
prostrates himself before the altar.

Liturgy of the Word   [p.77]
In addition to the exercises given in the Student Text, there could
also be a dramatic reading of the Passion, as on Palm Sunday, but
using the Gospel of John. Once again the division into parts will be
found in the Lectionary or in a Sunday Missal.

Veneration of the Cross   [p.77]
The aim of the veneration is to express love and gratitude to Christ
for his sacrifice which brought salvation. In the Middle Ages
people used to approach the cross on their knees, and it is still
traditional in some places for some people to genuflect one or
more times before venerating the Cross. It is also a gesture of faith,

repentance and adoration, directed towards Jesus Christ, the Saviour, whom the crucifix symbolizes.

Holy Communion   [p.78]
Mass itself is never celebrated on Good Friday in Catholic or Eastern Orthodox churches. Instead the people simply receive Holy Communion. They receive the Sacrament which was consecrated on Maundy Thursday and has been kept on the Altar of Repose. Because the Liturgy of Good Friday has some of the Characteristics of Mass, including a Liturgy of the Word and Holy Communion, but is a liturgy in which the Sacrament which is received has been 'pre-consecrated'; it used to be known, rather misleadingly, as 'Mass of the pre-sanctified'. This expression is no longer commonly used by Catholics, but the liturgy used in Orthodox churches on this day, and which they received from Pope Gregory The Great, is still referred to as 'the Liturgy of the Pre-sanctified'.

Aids
Catholic churches are traditionally well attended on Good Friday. The mood of the celebration is solemn and sombre, and it is difficult to reproduce or convey its impact in other settings and at other times. There is really no substitute for attendance at a celebration of the Solemn Liturgy. The text can be found in most Sunday Missals. For videos, see the notes at the end of this Unit.

Additional Note on Crucifixion
It may be helpful for pupils to know something about the nature and practice of crucifixion. The following are a few pertinent details.

Crucifixion was a form of execution regarded with horror by people of the ancient world. It was considered so terrible and degrading that it could not be inflicted on a Roman citizen, who instead would normally be executed by being garotted or beheaded. The Romans, however, used it as a means of executing other people who were guilty of particularly serious crimes. Among these would certainly be crimes of sedition and rebellion directed against Rome or the Emperor.

The one who was crucified was fixed to the horizontal beam by nails driven probably through his wrists, rather than the palms of his hands. Both feet were probably fixed to the vertical post by a single nail driven through both.

It was the fact that the victim was suspended from his outstretched arms which caused the particularly atrocious and prolonged agony of crucifixion. Anyone in this position finds breathing extremely difficult and laborious. In order to breath, he has constantly to push upwards with his legs against the nail through his feet, in order to raise his body to a position in which he can take a breath. Crucifixion was not simply a matter of hanging passively on the cross and bleeding to death. In fact, the bleeding was not the most important factor. Crucifixion entailed a constant tortured struggle. Death came about when the victim was no longer able to raise himself, or when his heart gave out under the strain. The process in fact could go on for many hours. In the end, people who were crucified died from suffocation or heart failure, rather than loss of blood in itself.

These considerations explain the practice of breaking the victim's legs, in order to hasten death, as recorded in the Gospel of John. This effectively stopped the victim pushing himself up to breathe, and so rapidly brought about his death.

4. Easter   [pp.79–89]

24:1–12 (The Empty Tomb)
Questions   [p.80]

1.   They had taken particular note of it, when they observed Jesus being placed in the tomb. (23:55).

2.   Mary Magdalene, Joanna, Mary the mother of James (24:10).

3.   They were 'in dazzling apparel'. Angels.

4.   Possibly 'they did not find the body', but more directly, 'Why do you seek the living among the dead?' (24:5).

5.   No, is the answer to the first question. No human being, as far as we know, is the answer to the second.

6.   Probably because they thought it was too incredible, or that they had imagined it because of their grief.

24:13–35 (The Road to Emmaus)
Questions   [p.81]

1.   They were not expecting Jesus to be alive. Perhaps there was something different about him. The text says, 'But their eyes were kept from recognising him.' Jesus wanted to choose the time and the circumstances when he would enable them to recognise him.

2.   Sad and disappointed (vv.17,21).

3.   He was 'mighty in deed and in word before God and all the people' (v.19).

4.   Yes. They had 'hoped that he was the one to redeem Israel'. This was what was expected of the Messiah.

5.   '... saying that they had even seen a vision of angels' (v.23).

6.   No. Some other disciples had seen it (v.24).

7.   See v.32.

8.   The main point is that the suffering and death of Jesus was the fulfilment of what was said in Scripture concerning the Christ.

9.   A variety of possibilities, e.g. the 'suffering servant' passage from Isaiah, Psalm 22.

10. The 'breaking of bread': the Last Supper, the Eucharist.

11. The Apostles. Only eleven now because one of them, Judas Iscariot, had killed himself (Mt 27:3–5).

12. Peter.

13. That they also could recognise and encounter Jesus in 'the breaking of bread', i.e. the celebration of the Eucharist.

24:36–53 (Jesus Appears to the Apostles)
Questions   [p.82]

1.   The reference to his 'hands and feet' (v.39).

2.   He invited the Apostles to touch him. He also ate with them.

3. He suddenly appeared among them (v.36).

4. He helped them to understand how the sufferings of Christ were foretold in the Scriptures.

5. Among the various possibilities, Psalm 22 is the most obvious.

6. He speaks here of his own suffering and Resurrection as the suffering and Resurrection of 'the Christ' (v.46).

7. Repentance and forgiveness, in the name of Jesus (v.47).

8. That they are preaching with Jesus's authority, as his witnesses.

9. Probably that Jesus's blessing remains with the Church, which continues to act in his name.

Something to Do [p.82]

The aim of this activity is to help pupils appreciate the tremendous impact on the Apostles and the early Church of the assurance that Jesus had risen from the dead, and the implications which the Resurrection had for them. It is an opportunity for pupils to consider why the Resurrection is important for Christians.

Evidence for the Resurrection [p.83]

This is not meant to be a 'proof', nor does it treat the matter exhaustively. It is merely a summary of some of the main points which emerge from the Scriptural testimony. It may serve as a starting point for discussion.

Easter—How The Church Celebrates [pp.84–89]

A full account of the Liturgy of the Easter Vigil and the Masses of Easter may be found in the Missal.

Holy Saturday, up to the Easter Vigil, is traditionally a time when the Church contemplates Christ buried in the tomb. Though in monasteries, religious houses and some churches the official Prayer of the Church (the 'Divine Office') is still celebrated, there is no celebration of Mass, and even the reception of Holy Communion outside Mass is forbidden, except for those who are in danger of death.

The Easter Vigil—The Service of Light [pp.85–86]
The Paschal Candle symbolizes the light of Christ—the light of truth and goodness and love—overcoming the darkness of evil and error. The entry of the Paschal Candle into the darkened church symbolizes the risen Christ dispelling the darkness of sin and death and bringing the light of his truth and salvation to the world. As the people's candles are lit from it, gradually that light spreads through the whole congregation. It is a sign that it is from Christ that the members of the Church receive his truth and the light of faith which enables them to accept it. It is also the sign that they share with him in the triumph of his Resurrection, and receive from him the new life which he brings. Christians are children of the light, called to walk in the light of Christ.

The Markings on the Paschal Candle
These are the markings which are traditionally made. They may be incised into the wax by the priest, but very commonly a decorated Cross and the Alpha and Omega symbols have previously been incorporated, either by means of a coloured moulding or by a transfer. In this case, the priest simply traces the outlines. The number of the year, which may be added as in the diagram, is however normally lightly incised with a sharp stylus.

The meaning of the Alpha and Omega symbol is given in the marginal note on p.85. The Cross and the incense grains, which represent the five wounds of Christ, are a reminder of the suffering and death through which Jesus passed to achieve salvation, and over which he triumphed in the Resurrection. The presence of these symbols of the Passion on the Paschal Candle emphasizes the necessary connection between Crucifixion and Resurrection as integral aspects of the one mystery of salvation in Jesus Christ. The 'incense grains' which are inserted in the Cross on the candle are very often encased in metal studs, each with a spike on the back of it. These spikes are inserted into the wax, in order to attach the 'grains' to the candle.

It may be possible for teachers to obtain an old Paschal Candle from a local Catholic Church, to bring into School. They may also be able to obtain examples of the kinds of candle which the people use during the Vigil.

Liturgy of the Word   [p.86]
The Readings may be found in the Lectionary or in a Sunday
Missal. Pupils should appreciate the significance of the obligatory
reading from Exodus. but are not expected to know the details of
the other readings or to be able to deal with questions concerning
the specific suitability of other individual lessons. They should,
however, have some general idea of the kind of themes which are
dealt with in the readings as a whole. One relatively quick way of
identifying the main point of each of the readings and the reason
why each is thought appropriate is to look at the prayer which
follows each. Pupils should know the significance of the Easter
Alleluia and the general content of the Gospel passage read in the
Easter Vigil Mass.

Baptismal Liturgy and Blessing of the Font   [p.87]
Baptism represents the communication to individuals of the
reconciliation and new life won for us by Jesus in his death and
resurrection. In Baptism, Christians believe that they, so to speak,
die with Christ, and rise with him to new life. That is why Easter is
especially associated with Baptism. In the early Church, Easter
was in fact the normal time for all baptisms to take place.

At the Vigil and the Masses of Easter Day the Nicene Creed is
omitted. Its place is taken by the renewal of the renunciation of sin
and profession of faith, as used in Baptism. This profession of faith
is, in fact, basically the 'Apostles' Creed' split up into sections and
put into question form. The Apostles' Creed is the name given to
the profession of faith which, with only comparatively minor
variations, has been used as the Baptismal Creed of the Roman
Church from very ancient times.

After the blessing of the Baptismal water, the holy water stoups in
the church, which were emptied for Good Friday, are refilled.
Catholics customarily dip their fingers in this water as they enter
and/or leave Church, and make the sign of the cross on themselves
with it. This is a constant reminder of their baptism.

The Renewal of Baptismal Commitment at the Masses on Easter
Sunday is primarily intended for those who did not attend the
Easter Vigil, though all take part in it. Many Catholics in fact
attend both.

Things To Do   [p.89]
These activities are intended to be useful for revision purposes.

Videos

There are a variety of videos and other audio/visual aids which
might be helpful for one or more aspects of this Unit. Below are
given just a few examples of videos which teachers may find
useful. So that teachers may themselves assess their suitability and
the way in which any may be best incorporated into the teaching
programme, prior inspection is highly advisable.

Passion and Resurrection

• *The Life of Jesus*, in four parts, part 3 on the Passion, part 4 on
  the Resurrection. Each of these two parts lasts about 10 minutes.
  It is not tied to the Gospel of Luke (which may pose problems),
  but may be found useful as general background introduction.
  (Catholic Video Education, Clare Priory, Clare, Suffolk CO10
  8NX.Tel. 01787 278385)

• *The Passion of Christ*, a traditional dramatic presentation of the
  Passion from the Last Supper to Emmaus. Scripturally based,
  but not tied to Luke, it lasts nineteen minutes and might be
  useful as general background or overview. (Veritas Book and
  Video Distribution, Lower Avenue, Leamington Spa,
  Warwickshire CV31 3NP. Tel. 01926 451730)

• *The Gospel according to Luke*, a pack of four videos (No. 4
  of which concerns the Passion and Resurrection). It is a
  reasonably priced American dramatized presentation, with a
  'voice-over' giving the whole text of Luke (Authorized
  Version). (Island Videos — obtainable only at retail outlets of
  W. H. Smith)

Passover

• *Pesah—The Jewish Feast of Passover*, a video of a Jewish
  family celebrating Passover. This is, of course, concerned with
  contemporary practice, rather than the situation at the time of
  Jesus, but it may be found useful as general background.
  (Veritas Book and Video Distribution, address as above)

Celebration of Holy Week and Easter

- *Easter* highlights the main theological and liturgical points of the Catholic celebration of Easter, and lasts 40 minutes. (Ref. V43, Catholic Truth Society, 192 Vauxhall Bridge Road, London SW1V 1PD)
- *Easter* (Rev. E. Swayne) deals with the main theological and liturgical points of the Catholic celebration of Easter, and lasts 60 minutes. (Veritas Video, obtainable from Veritas Book and Video Distribution, address as above)
- *Holy Week and Easter* deals with the symbolism and meaning of Holy Week, and lasts 28 minutes. (Obtainable from Veritas Book and Video Distribution; address as above)

The Celebration of Easter in the Byzantine Rite

Preliminary Notes

In an Orthodox church, or any church of the Byzantine Rite, the sanctuary in which the altar ('Holy Table') stands, is separated from the body of the church by a screen in which are set icons. This is known as the Iconostasis. In the middle of the Iconostasis are doors which are opened at certain points in the ritual.

Holy Week, as in the Latin Rite, is preceded by Lent, which is a period of fasting. During Holy Week, as in the Latin Rite, there are distinctive celebrations of Maundy Thursday and Good Friday.

The celebration of the liturgical services is carried out in its fullest form in monasteries. In ordinary churches, adaptations are made to meet the circumstances of an ordinary parish. In addition, there are some typical variations in customary practice between various national churches, particularly between the Greeks and Russians. Some churches, which observe the Byzantine rite are in full communion with Rome, and are therefore distinct from the Orthodox Church, though their rites are very similar. One example is the Ukrainian Catholic Church. These are Eastern rite Catholics, as distinct from the more numerous 'Latin rite' Catholics who follow the liturgy of the Roman rite. All are fully members of the Catholic Church.

The Celebration of Easter
The celebration of Easter begins on Holy Saturday, and reaches a
high point at a service starting at Midnight, at the very beginning
of Easter Day.

Holy Saturday
In the Byzantine rite, Holy Saturday commemorates not only
Christ's entombment, but also his entry into the world of the dead
to set free the souls of the just. On the previous day, Good Friday,
a central feature has been a shroud, representing the shroud of
Christ, placed in a raised position in the middle of the church. This
is subsequently placed as a covering onto the altar, so that the
Easter Mass may be celebrated over it. Among the Greeks this is
done on Good Friday itself, but the Russians keep the shroud in the
middle of the church until the evening of Holy Saturday, and then
place it on the altar.

Earlier in the day there is celebrated the Office of Vespers, which
includes fifteen readings from the Old Testament. The clergy then
change from black vestments into white, and a preliminary
proclamation of the Resurrection is made, first in hymns, then
through the Gospel of the Resurrection. In the celebration of the
Eucharist which follows, the Liturgy of St Basil is used. After
Mass, at least in monasteries, the whole of the Acts of the Apostles
is read.

Easter—Midnight Vigil and First Mass of Easter
At midnight on Holy Saturday, just as Easter Day is beginning, the
priests come out from the sanctuary carrying lights, and then they
and the congregation, who may also carry lighted candles, circle
the darkened church, in imitation of the women coming to the
tomb on the first Easter morning.

They knock on the closed doors of the Church, which symbolize
the entry to the tomb. Then the doors are opened and the priests
enter, chanting 'Christ is risen from the dead.' The icon of the
risen Christ is incensed.

Then comes the Office of Matins, during which, at set intervals,
the priests exchange the Easter greeting with the people: 'Christ is
risen'; 'He is risen indeed'.

A special homily of St John Chrysostom is read, in which the theme is that even those who have not shared in the Lenten fast can join in the celebration of Easter. The joy of the Resurrection is for everyone, even if they come to it at the last minute. In the celebration of the Eucharist which follows, the Liturgy of St John Chrysostom is used.

Easter Day
Nowadays, in Orthodox churches situated in the West, the custom of also celebrating Mass later in the day has often been adopted. The traditional main service, however, is the celebration of Vespers. One interesting feature is that the Easter Gospel is proclaimed in a number of different languages, as a sign that the joy and the message of the Resurrection is for everyone.

There is no exact equivalent of the Paschal Candle in the Byzantine rite, but a similar contrast between light and darkness is used. Both Byzantine and Latin rites employ a night service, in which the contrast can be made clear. In both rites, the proclamation of the Resurrection in hymns and chants and through the reading of the Gospel is central.

The Byzantine rite does not have the custom of omitting 'alleluia' during Lent. Therefore the singing of 'alleluia' at Easter does not have the same significance.

The readings, psalms, chants etc. used in the Vespers of Holy Saturday and the Midnight office of Matins roughly correspond in spirit and function to the Liturgy of the Word at the Latin rite Easter Vigil. Both the Latin Easter Vigil and the Byzantine midnight service involve the celebration of the first Mass of Easter.

The Byzantine Vigil in particular seeks to promote a feeling of actually taking part in the original occurrence.

Inexpensive copies of the services of Holy Week may be obtained from the Russian Orthodox Cathedral of the Assumption and All Saints, Ennismore Gardens, London, SW7 1NH.

UNIT 3 (Alternative A)

THE PUBLIC MINISTRY OF JESUS
ACCORDING TO ST LUKE

Unit 3 allows Centres a choice. Alternative A contains St Luke's version of the Public Ministry of Jesus. The syllabus orders the material according to a number of themes (Syllabus, pages 24–25). For convenience, the Student Text follows the order of the syllabus and it is recommended that the material is taught in that order.

Methodology
Refer to the General Notes on Methodology. With particular reference to Unit 3A, many ideas for presenting the material are suggested in the Student Text. Activities such as discussion, drama, role-play, poster-making should not be despised as vehicles for learning.

Aims of the Unit
- To help pupils become familiar with the relevant texts from Luke's Gospel.
- To help the pupils relate the texts to present-day situations.

1. *Prelude* [pp.97–101]

Questions (first set) [p.98]

1. Bear fruits that befit repentance.

2. ... do not begin to say to yourselves, 'We have Abraham for our father'; for I tell you, God is able from these stones to raise up children to Abraham.

3. John is comparing God to a woodman. A woodman uses an axe to cut down a tree that does not bear good fruit, then he burns it in a fire. In a similar way God will deal with people who are wicked. The fire represents hell.

Exercise
The answer is in 3:11–14. Pupils are asked to write it in their own words—their answer should indicate their understanding of each of the sections of John's answer.

Questions (second set)

1. The Christ (or Messiah), whom John identifies as Jesus. Some of those present thought John might be the Christ, but he is anxious to make it clear that he is not.

2. '... he who is mightier than I is coming, the thong of whose sandals I am not worthy to untie.'

3. Through Jesus, people will be able to receive God's Holy Spirit. Jesus's baptism will not be a mere calling to repentance like John's; the recipients will be given a share in the very life of God. Fire is a powerful symbol of the Spirit as the purifying and energising gift through whom Christians are cleansed, and from whom they receive the strength and power to fight evil.

4. (a) Using heavy sticks or batons, the farmer beats the ears of (in this case) wheat in order to separate the grains of wheat from the outer husks or chaff. Threshing floors were (and still are in Israel) prepared outside a town or village by removing the grass, and top-soil of an area large enough for the peoples needs. The hard, bare rock is thus exposed and used for threshing.
    (b) Using a special kind of tool called a winnowing-fork (or fan, because it is shaped rather like a fan), the farmer throws the threshed wheat straight up into the air. Being heavier than the chaff, the grain itself falls back to the ground in more or less the same place as it was before. The husks are blown a short distance by the wind and form a neat pile nearby. These are sometimes used for pig-food (though, of course, neither Jews nor Muslims would keep pigs) or they are burned.

5. 'His winnowing fork' refers to God. John is comparing the wheat to good people, the chaff to the wicked and the unquenchable fire to hell. At the end of time, God would separate the good from the wicked.

6. Doing his best to persuade them to do as he wished (in this case to repent and accept his baptism as a sign of that repentance).

7. The word GOSPEL means 'Good News.' It is the Good News that the Christ (Messiah) was amongst them and about to offer salvation to those who sought and accepted it in repentance.

Temptation in the Wilderness (4:1–13)   [p.100]
Questions (left-hand side)

1.   The Israelites (under Moses) wandered 40 years in the desert
      before entering the promised land (Exod 12 ff.), and Moses
      himself spent 40 days and nights in the presence of God on
      Mount Sinai when he received the Ten Commandments (cf.
      Deut 9:9). The Prophet Elijah journeyed for 40 days and
      nights to Mount Horeb, to converse with God (I Kings 19:8).

2.   Similarities:
      - Forty years in the desert.   Forty days and nights in the
        Moses spending 40 days on   desert.
        Mount Sinai.

      - The people asked for bread;   The devil tried to tempt
        the next day they discovered   Jesus to change stones on
        a bread-like substance,   the ground into bread.
        manna, lying on the ground.

      - Moses found God on the   The devil took Jesus to the
        high place—at the top of   highest point of the temple:
        Mount Sinai.   the Jews believed that the
                                            temple was God's earthly
                                            dwelling place.

      Elijah, the Prophet:
      - journeyed for 40 days and nights;
      - on the strength of food he had received from God;
      - encountered God on the top of Mount Horeb (I Kings
        19:4–14).

Questions (right-hand side)
- Pride. To seek for fame, glory and perhaps to wallow in a
  feeling of self-importance. To seek to establish the Kingdom by
  wrong means, or by compromising with evil.
- He wants to be a humble Messiah, leading the people to a love
  of God. One who thinks nothing of worldly power, or vanity,
  and who wants only to do God's will.

Looking Back—Revision Exercises   [p.101]

1.   Gentile Christians. (See p.94 for an amplification of this
      answer).

2. 'At a glance.'

3. The information given to the pupils is to be found on p.93. 'Q' is the material not found in Mark's Gospel but common to Matthew's and Luke's Gospels. Scholars think there must have been a source (hence 'Q' = 'Quelle' = 'source' in German), now lost, to which Mark did not have access but which was available to both Matthew and Luke. Because the material is so similar (word for word in many cases), scholars believe the source to have been a written one.

4. The probable answers most will give are the Good Samaritan and the Prodigal Son. However, there are at least 17! Any two of the following are therefore acceptable: The Moneylender 7:41–43; The Good Samaritan 10:30–37; A Friend in Need 11:5–8; The Rich Fool 12:16–21; The Watchful Servants 12:35–40; The Faithful Servant 12:42–48; The Unfruitful Fig Tree 13:6–9; The Best Places at a Wedding Feast 14:7–14; The Great Feast and the Reluctant Guests 14:16–24; Counting the cost 14:28–33; The Lost Coin 15:8–10; The Prodigal Son 15:11–32; The Shrewd Manager 16:1–8; The Rich Man and Lazarus 16:19–31; The Master and his Servant 17:7–10; The Widow and the Judge 18:2–5; The Pharisee and the Tax Collector 18:10–14.

5. Acts of the Apostles (p.94)

6. These are listed on p.94. Any three!

7. He writes in excellent Greek, takes care over the way he presents his material—he is often very poetic and dramatic. Further evidence is the probability that he was a medical doctor. Again, see p.94 for a further explanation.

8. He often emphasises the healing ministry of Jesus and often describes illness in more detail than the other Evangelists. Refer to page 94 for a fuller answer.

9. Tiberius Caesar (Luke 3:1).

10. At the time of the preaching of John the Baptist, Caiaphas was the High Priest. However, his father-in-law was Annas who had previously been High Priest. Possibly Caiaphas

suffered a great deal of interference from Annas in trying to fulfil his duties! (p.97)

11. See Luke 3:4b–6.

12. 'You brood of vipers! Who warned you to flee from the wrath to come?' (3:7b)

13. 'Turning back'. (p.97)

14. (a) 'Collect no more than is appointed you.' (Luke 3:13)
    (b) 'Rob no one by violence or by false accusation, and be content with your wages.' (Luke 3:14b)

15. 'His winnowing-fork' refers to God. John is comparing the threshing floor to the world, his granary to heaven, the wheat to good people, the chaff to the wicked and the unquenchable fire to hell. At the end of time, God would separate the good from the wicked, the former would live in heaven and the latter would burn in the everlasting fire of hell.

16. Initially, he had John imprisoned. Later Herod had him beheaded at the request of the daughter of Herodias. The details are to be found in Mark 6:14–29 (or a shorter version in Matthew 14:1–12).

17. The answer is to be found in Luke 3:21–22.
    THE FATHER: The heaven is opened ... and a voice came from heaven....
    THE SON: This is Jesus who has just been baptised and is now praying.
    THE HOLY SPIRIT: ... and the Holy Spirit descended upon him in bodily form, as a dove....

18. 'Thou art my beloved Son; with thee I am well pleased. (3:22b)

19. Because Christians believe that Jesus's father is God. Joseph, being betrothed to Mary, was Jesus's 'foster father.' However, during Jesus's childhood and until the start of his public ministry, people would suppose Joseph to be his father.

20. Adam (3:38): see p.99 of the Student Text.

2. The Galilean Ministry [pp.102–107]

Questions [p.104]

1. He gave them power and authority over all demons and to cure diseases. (9:1)

2. He told them to preach the kingdom of God and to heal. (9:2)

3. Because, in exchange for preaching the Gospel, they were to rely on the hospitality of the people amongst whom they served—they would discover that they were given whatever they needed.

4. To accept the hospitality that is first offered to them—not, for example, to move from this first household to what they might consider a better one!

5. To show that they cut off any association with them. The people of the town had been offered salvation and had rejected it. Shaking off the dust was a sign that they would have nothing to do further with that town—that they would not even carry some of the town's dust on their shoes!

6. To prepare them for the time when he would no longer be with them bodily and to show them what they would be able to do if they acted in his name.

7. The good news that the Kingdom of God was at hand.

The Transfiguration [p.106]
It is worth noting that the connection of Jesus with Moses and Elijah had been suggested in the account of Jesus' temptation in the wilderness (see notes above on questions on p.100). Jesus is the fulfilment of all that is represented by Moses and Elijah.

Looking Back—Revision Exercises [p.107]

1. The prophet Isaiah.

2. He has been anointed: to preach good news to the poor; to proclaim release to captives and the recovery of sight to the blind; to liberate the oppressed; etc.

3. He was the subject of the prophecy.

4. He criticized them, and refused to perform miracles for them.

5.   Simon (Peter), James and John.

6.   He was overawed by the great catch of fish, and felt unworthy.

7.   See marginal note on p.102 of the Student Text.

8.   'Rock'.

9.   Levi. (See p.103)

10. Basically because they were Jews working for the Romans, and they overcharged their fellow Jews in order to make a very comfortable living for themselves. A fuller answer is given in the margin of p.103.

11. Two named Simon, two named Jude, two named James, two brothers Andrew and John; Matthew, Philip, Bartholomew, Thomas. Again, a fuller answer is to be found in the Student Text p.103. (Luke 6:14–16)

12. 'One who is sent.' (p.103)

13. (a) Simon (not Peter); (b) Andrew; (c) Judas Iscariot.

14. They were a symbol of the Twelve Tribes of Israel. A fuller explanation is given in in the margin of p.103.

15. Briefly: take nothing for your journey, stay in the first house in which you are offered hospitality, shake the dust off your feet where you are not welcomed. The full account is in Luke 9:2–5.

16. John the Baptist; Elijah, one of the old prophets has risen. (Luke 9:19)

17. Peter.

18. 'The Anointed One.'

19. (a) The Old Testament Law or *Torah*.
     (b) The Old Testament Prophets. (p.106)

20. He was the fulfilment of the Law and the prophets. God's revelation was now complete. (p.106)

3.   Cures and Other Miracles   [pp.108–117]

On a Sabbath day Jesus Heals a Man with an Unclean
Spirit in the Synagogue (4:31–37)   [p.109]

Questions

1.   The miracle was a demonstration of the power of God and
      therefore of the arrival of the kingdom. The Jews were the
      Chosen People. Because of this, it was their privilege to be
      the first to be offered salvation. Only then would salvation be
      offered the Gentiles.

2.   It was fitting that the arrival of the kingdom should be made
      public on a sabbath (the Lord's day), in the presence of the
      local Jewish leaders. Jesus is 'Lord of the sabbath' and he
      was not to be limited by the rules about the sabbath that the
      Pharisees had developed.

3.   The symbolism is obvious—the reign of the devil (by whom
      this man is possessed) is being broken and the reign of the
      kingdom of God will take its place.

4.   No, he was not praising him! But he did recognise him and
      was afraid because he understood the significance of what
      Jesus was about to do.

5.   'The word' was Jesus's rebuke to the devil: 'Be silent and
      come out of him!' (4:35)

6.   The kingdom of God is greater than that of the devil, and
      so the evil spirits crumble under God's power. Because
      this evil spirit succumbs to Jesus's words, it is obvious to
      the bystanders that Jesus's authority and power are from .
      God.

Questions (first set)   [p.110]

1.   An exorcism.

2.   Refer to the pattern on p.110:
      (1) The situation is presented (4:33–34);
      (2) Not applicable;
      (3) Verse 35;
      (4) Verses 36–37.

Cure of Peter's Mother-in-law (4:38–30)

Questions (second set)

1. That he was either married at the time or he had been married previously. Some think he was widower at the time Jesus met him.

2. That it was a *high* fever. (Mark simply refers to it as a fever). (See p.94.)

3. Refer to the pattern on left hand side of page:
    (1) Now Simon's mother-in-law was ill with a high fever,
    (2) and they besought him for her.
    (3) And he stood over her and rebuked the fever, and it left her;
    (4) and immediately she rose and served them.

4. Simply because she was ill. He was able to help, and so he did.

Cure of the Man with a Withered Hand (6:6–11) [p.112]

Questions (first set)

1. Again, probably because the man was disabled, Jesus was able to help and so he wanted to. However, in this case it was also to make the point to the scribes and Pharisees that God was not interested in their petty rules that forbade healing on the sabbath. Jesus, being himself of God, and therefore 'Lord of the sabbath' knew God's mind in this matter.

2. Perhaps, because he was attentive to detail—especially if he was, as many scholars think, a doctor—and so interested in detail concerning medical matters.

3. Because they had been humiliated by Jesus who healed the man against their (tacit yet real) opposition. As far as they were concerned, work—which includes healing—was forbidden on the sabbath day. Jesus had ignored this and so was undermining their authority.

4. Harm. Because, on account of their petty rules, they were preventing good (healing) from taking place and they were not able to know that this was not what God wanted.

5.   A miracle of healing (see the categories on p.110).

Cure of the Centurion's Slave (7:1–10)

Questions (second set)

1.   (a) It does! (Check it against the pattern on p.110.)
     (b) A healing miracle. It is different from usual however, because the cure takes place from a distance.

2.   Because of his interest in both Gentiles and in the 'underdog'. He wanted everyone to know that Jesus's salvation was for all people, no matter what their background.

3.   Just before Holy Communion: 'Lord, I am not worthy to receive you, but only say the word and I shall be healed.'

4.   He was showing that he believed Jesus to have the same authority over sickness and disease that he had over the soldiers under his command.

5.   This man was a Gentile, a Roman soldier, and yet he showed more faith in Jesus than the Jews ('Israel') who boasted that their knowledge and love of God was greater than that of anyone else. These Jews had not recognised Jesus's true identity but the Roman soldier had!

6.   Illness *represented* sin (in fact it was commonly believed that it was the direct result of sin). This miracle demonstrates the power of God over the forces of evil. The kingdom of the devil was being overcome by the kingdom of Heaven. By the healing miracles in general, Jesus was demonstrating:
     (a) that the kingdom of Heaven was now being established;
     (b) that it was not exclusively for the Jews.

The Calming of The Storm (8:22–25)   [p.113]

Questions (first set)

1.   It does!

2.   Someone with the power and authority of God. They seem to have realised who he was!

The Raising of Jairus's Daughter etc (8:40–46)

Questions (second set)

1. In both cases, *faith*. '... Daughter, your faith has made you well ...' (v.48), and '... only believe, and she shall be well ...' (v.50).

2. Pupils should have looked for medical details such as; 'she was dying' (v.42); '... a woman who had a flow of blood for twelve years' (v.43); 'could not be cured by anyone' (also v.43).

3. Peter, John and James. The Transfiguration.

Cure of an Epileptic Demoniac (9:37–43) [p.115]

Questions (first set)

1. Eighteen years.

2. The ruler of the synagogue.

3. For healing on the sabbath—we have already seen that this was against the Jewish Law because it was considered to be work.

4. Because they also work on the sabbath by untying an ox and leading it to water.

5. A Jewess—a member of God's chosen people.

6. ' ... whom Satan bound for eighteen years...' (v.16).

The Ten Lepers (17:11–19) [p.116]

Questions

1. Because of his special interest in the fact that Jesus's salvation was offered to all—even those who were considered outcasts by the 'righteous' Jews. (See General Notes on Luke's Gospel, Student Text, p.94.)

2. '... fell on his face at Jesus' feet, giving him thanks.' (Luke 17:16)

3. His faith (v.19)

4. Samaritans were hated by the Jews because they had intermarried with the pagans; they nevertheless claimed to be

true Jews. The Jews of Judaea considered that Samaritans were traitors to Israel, hence the hatred. In this story, it was one of these 'inferior' Jews who proved to be the best!

5.　Not to be racist. People of other races are not inferior. Not to be prejudiced on the grounds of race, nationality or religion.

Essay Question
The best idea would probably be simply to set the essay and see how the pupils fare. Alternatively, these notes could be given to them as a skeleton outline.

- Jesus usually performed miracles simply because he had compassion on the people he was with and so he wished to exercise the power to heal which had come from God. The miracles also served to demonstrate God's power over the forces of evil and therefore the arrival of the kingdom of God.

- The second part is straightforward enough.

- Pupils will probably think in terms of places of pilgrimages such as Lourdes. They may not realise that the Church still requires proof of miracles as part of the canonisation process. These miracles arise from intercession through the (dead) person concerned and are ordinary, daily-life situations, e.g. prayer in an ordinary parish Church.

Revision Exercises　　　　　　　　　　　　　　　　　　[p.117]

1.　Ruled by God (p.108).

2.　*The* Anointed One (also p.108).

3.　He would be a warrior-king and would lead an army against the occupying power (in this case, the Romans) and establish God's kingdom in Israel for all time. (again, p.108)

4.　See the explanation given on right-hand side of p.108.

5.　The rejoicing with God at the end of time for those who had demonstrated their love for him and so had become members of the kingdom of God, i.e. Heaven (again, p.108).

6.　Because healing was considered to be work and was against the Law (*Torah*). The Law was based on the third commandment, 'Remember to keep holy the sabbath day.'

7. They are listed on p.110.

8. He often touched them in some way. For example, in the case of Jairus's daughter he 'took her by the hand.' In the case of the woman suffering from a 'flow of blood', she touched him (or rather the fringe of this garment). In the case of the Centurion's Slave, as far as we know, Jesus did not even meet the slave. He cured him at a distance by simply saying 'a word'. He often said some-thing like, 'Go, your faith has cured you.'

9. The pattern is to be found on p.110.

10. The resurrection of the body from the dead (p.111).

11. Temple worship. (again p.111).

12. The Essenes.

13. The Man with an Unclean Spirit (4:31–37), *or*
The Man with a Withered Hand (6:6–11), *or*
The Crippled Woman (13:10–17)

14. Lord.

15. 'I tell you, not even in Israel have I found such faith.' (7:9b)

16. See the explanations on p.113.

17. The connection between sin and sickness: They believed that sickness was the direct consequence of sin. See p.113 for a fuller explanation.

18. Several are suggested on p.114. Pupils should simply choose one of them.

19. According to the *Torah* only the priests could declare them to be clean again (Leviticus 14:1–32). The answer for the pupils is on p.116).

20. He was a Samaritan. (17:16b)

4. The Sermon on the Plain [p118-120]

Love of Enemies (6:27–36)

Questions (first set) [p.119]

1. (a) do good,
    (b) bless them,
    (c) pray for them,
    (d) give him your coat as well,
    (e) give to everyone who does so. (6:27–30)

2. Two of the following:
    - Love those who love them.
    - Do good to those who do good to them.
    - Lend to those from whom they hope to receive. (6:32–34)

3. The answer is found in v.35, '... your reward will be great, and you will be sons of the Most High'.

4. Because their Father (God) is merciful. (v.36)

About Judging Others (6:37–42)

Questions (second set)

1. A blind man has to be guided by someone who can see. In the same way a person wishing to go to heaven has to be led by someone who knows the way—who can *see* the way. The disciple is led by his teacher. Jesus is *the* teacher, but in time, when they have sufficiently learned this *way* for themselves, his disciples will become teachers and lead others.

2. The 'speck' is a small fault. The 'log' is a much greater fault. Jesus is saying, get rid of the big faults in your life first before you can qualify to advise others about theirs.

Exercise [p.120]
Answers will vary. The following are ideas, but are not exhaustive. Christians should try to live in harmony with those amongst whom they live and work. They should not be the initiators of quarrels or fights and when these occur, they should try to resolve them amicably. They should be prepared to help anyone who either asks or requires such help. They should help to look after the poor and needy. They should always be willing to forgive.

Looking Back. Revision Exercises

1. Any one from those listed in 6:17.

2. It was the style whereby a rabbi moved quickly from one theme to another. It was used to prevent boredom and to keep the people's interest. See p.118.

3. '... for yours is the kingdom of God.' (6:20)

4. '... for you shall hunger.' (6:25)

5. 'As you wish that men would do to you, do so to them.' (6:31)

6. Because even sinners do so! (6:32)

7. 'Judge not, and you will not be judged.' (6:37a)

8. The 'speck' is small fault. The 'log' is a much greater fault. Jesus is saying, get rid of the big faults in your life first before you can qualify to advise others about theirs.

9. The answer is to be found on p.120. Note also that good trees bear good fruit, bad trees produce either bad fruit or none at all and so are worthless. It is the same with people. Their 'fruits' are their actions. Those who lead good and useful lives, doing good to and for those around them, are those who bear good fruit. These are worthy people. Those whose deeds are evil are those who bear bad or no fruit. They are worthless people.

10. Actions! (See p.120.)

5. *Parables and Other Teaching*   [pp.121–134]

The Woman who was a Sinner (7:36–50)

Questions   [p.121]

1. The answer is in verses 37–38. She brought an alabaster flask of ointment, stood behind him at his feet weeping, she wet his feet with her tears and dried them with her hair, kissed his feet and anointed them with ointment.

2. Because she was a well-known sinner and it was not seemly for decent people to have anything to do with the likes of her!

3.	The one who owed more was the more grateful to have his debts forgiven; similarly with sinners. Everyone is a sinner but God is ready to forgive those who repent. It might be harder for those who are the greater sinners (e.g. this woman) to repent—but such people would afterwards have the greater love for God.

4.	Only God could forgive sins and therefore think of Jesus as being God himself.

5.	'Your faith has saved you, go in peace.' (7:50)

The Good Samaritan (10:25–37)

Questions   [p.122]

1.	Because the hero (the Samaritan) was a despised Samaritan.

2.	'... and he went to him, and bound up his wounds, pouring on oil and wine.' (v.34)

3.	As in No. 2, but also the following: he put him on his own beast, took him to an inn and took care of him. Next day he paid the innkeeper to look after him and promised to pay any extra necessary on his return.

4.	'Your neighbour is anybody at all, regardless of things like class or nationality—especially if he/she is in need.

The Prodigal Son (15:11–32)

Questions   [p.123]

1.	'... he squandered his property in loose living.' (15:13b)

2.	'I will arise and go to my father, and I will say to him, "Father, I have sinned against heaven and against you; I am no longer worthy to be called your son; treat me as one of your hired servants." ' (15:18)

3.	God.

4.	'But while he was yet at a distance, his father saw him and had compassion, and ran and embraced him and kissed him.' (15:20b)

5.	He '... said to his servants, "Bring quickly the best robe, and put it on him; and put a ring on his hand, and shoes on his feet; and bring the fatted calf and kill it, and let us eat and make merry." ' (15:22–23)

6. 'Lo, these many years I have served you, and I have never disobeyed your command; yet you never gave me a kid, that I might make merry with my friends. But when this son of yours came, who has devoured your living with harlots, you killed for him the fatted calf!' (15:29–30)

7. God will welcome back anyone, no matter how great their sin, as long as he/she repents and resolves to reform.

Zacchaeus the Tax Collector (19:1–10)

Questions (first set) [p.124]

1. Because the main character is a tax collector—one of Luke's 'minority groups' for whom Jesus brings salvation no less than for the pious Jews.

2. Because he was interested in associating not with the 'good' people but with this dreadful sinner, a tax collector.

3. Because Zacchaeus had repented and had decided to put right his past sins according to the requirements of the *Torah*.

The Pharisee and the Tax Collector (18:9–14)

Questions (second set)

1. He fasted twice a week. He gave tithes of all that he got. (18:12)

2. 'But the tax collector, standing far off, would not even lift up his eyes to heaven, but beat his breast, saying, "God, be merciful to me a sinner!" ' (18:13)

3. To show that it is what people are like at heart that is important in God's eyes, not external appearances. People who seem outwardly more virtuous than others may actually be less pleasing to God.

4. Be humble. Do not despise others—they may be better than you in God's eyes. Be sure that if you do good, you do it for the right reasons.

The Woman who Followed Jesus (8:1–3)

Questions [p.125]

1. He was going 'through the cities and villages, preaching and bringing the good news of the kingdom of God'.

2. The twelve apostles.

3. They would have bought food, clothes and other material necessities for them out of their own money. They were probably quite wealthy.

The Parable of the Sower explained (8:11–15)

Questions [p.126]

1. '... those who, when they hear the word, receive it with joy, but these have no root, they believe for a while and in time of temptation fall away.' (v.13)

2. '... they are those who hear, but as they go on their way they are choked by the cares and riches and pleasures of life, and their fruit does not mature.' (v.14)

3. '... they are those who, hearing the word, hold it fast in an honest and good heart, and bring forth fruit with patience.' (v.15)

4. The people concerned have been deceived or corrupted by the power of evil into rejecting or abandoning faith in the word.

5. Examples include those who become or are too anxious to become rich, or become obsessed with possessions or their business to the extent that they neglect religion and their spiritual life.

6. Those who responsibly attend to their religious duties, and pray regularly. In addition they meticulously look after their neighbours—especially those in need; do all they can to help their fellow human beings, and in general seek to imitate Christ in their lives. Many pupils might mention a particular person in their neighbourhood or parish. Many will probably have someone like Mother Teresa of Calcutta in mind.

Exercises

Because a wide variety of answers is possible, model answers to these two questions are not being offered.

First Prediction of the Passion (9:22–26)

Questions [p.127]

1. 'Come after me' means being a disciple of—doing the work that Jesus is doing'. 'Deny himself' means making sacrifices. 'Take up his cross daily' means accepting the difficulties and trials that following Jesus involves. In other words, Jesus cannot and does not promise that being a Christian will be an easy life—very often it will be the opposite. His followers must be prepared for this.

2. Whoever makes sacrifices in this life in order to follow Jesus and do his work will gain eternal life in heaven. In particular, this is so for those who literally sacrifice their life in order to be faithful to Jesus.

3. The most important thing is to possess God's eternal life in his kingdom. This life is only a temporary phase in a person's existence—how, then, would a person profit by gaining many material possessions and great wealth if s/he then lost his/her chance of eternal life?

4. He, in turn, will be ashamed of them on judgement day at the end of time.

5. Difficult. Followers of Jesus are expected to be prepared to sacrifice everything in order to follow him faithfully.

Sacrifices Needed in Following Jesus (9:57–62)

Questions (first set) [p.128]

1. They used the title 'Lord', *'Kyrie'* in Greek (9:59 and 61).

2. Himself. The title 'Son of man' is the title he usually used for himself.

3. Something like: 'Go and tell people that the Messiah (the Christ) has arrived', or 'Go and tell people that their salvation is here'.

Martha and Mary 10:38–42

Questions (second set)

1. Mary.

2. 'Martha was distracted with much serving....' (10:40)

3. This is the Divine title again. Martha recognises Jesus's divine status, and so does Luke. He stresses the fact by using the title several times in this short passage.

4. To love and serve the Lord (God).

Question

For example, by helping, or giving to (or fund-raising for) a charity that does this work. (*Note:* In the text for the parable of the Banquet, pupils are referred back to the notes on the Parable of the Marriage Feast on p.124.)

The Lord's Prayer (11:1–4)

Exercise   [p.129]

1. God.

2. May God be worshipped and honoured.

3. May God's Kingdom be finally established.

4. Give us all that we truly need.

5. They are linking their prayer for forgiveness to their own readiness to forgive others. This should remind them throughout their lives to show forgiveness for the transgressions of others.

6. 'Save us from temptation', the temptation to belong to Satan's kingdom rather than God's.

Parable of the Friend at Midnight 11:5–13

Question
Faith. A belief that God is there and that he will always answer our prayers. For his own reasons, God does not always answer our prayers immediately, but he will eventually and so persistence is worthwhile.

Activities (Margin)

The following are a few examples of Jesus at prayer. Teachers should use their professional judgement in crediting other examples:

- At his baptism. (3:21)
- After he healed a leper, others came to be healed, but he withdrew to the wilderness to pray. (5:16)
- Just before selecting twelve apostles from amongst his disciples he spent the night in prayer. (6:12)
- Jesus prayed immediately before he asked his disciples 'Who do people say that I am?' (9:18)
- At the Transfiguration. (9:28)
- Jesus was praying immediately before the disciples asked Him to teach them how to pray. (11:1)
- He prayed on the Mount of Olives on the night before he died. (22:41)

The great gift which Jesus says God will certainly give those who ask is the Holy Spirit. (4.11:13)

Possible reasons why some prayer appears to be unanswered are:

1. to test the person's faith—will s/he give up or persist? (as in the parable of the Judge and the Widow)

2. God answers prayer by giving us what we *need*—this is not always the same as what we *want*! Thus, God may answer our prayer, but not in the way we expect and so the temptation is sometimes to suppose he hasn't answered our prayer at all.

3. there are some prayers that cannot be answered (even by God!)—for example, on a particular summer's day, a farmer prays for rain as his crops need them and some Cub-Scouts pray for sunshine as they are going on an outing. Both prayers cannot be answered. (However, it rains and the Cubs still had a good time, then *perhaps* God *did* answer their prayer but not in the way they expected!—see No.2, above!) In addition some people may pray for not only what is not good for them, but for something which is wrong.

In general, God may answer prayer by saying yes, no, or not yet. Christians believe that if we pray in faith, God will only say 'No' in order to give us something better, something more truly beneficial.

Parable of the Rich Fool (12:13–21)

Questions (first set) [p.130]

1. The way in which he has demonstrated his love for God and for his fellow human beings, is one possible answer.

2. 'Tonight you will die.'

3. He has demonstrated little or no love for God and so has put aside few, if any, spiritual treasures against his eternal life.

4. Perhaps those who neglect their duties towards God (even, perhaps denying his existence) or their neighbours, but attach great importance to material things instead. Thus, they amass many riches, perhaps at the expense of the basic needs of the poor.

Trust In Providence (12:22–32)

Questions (second set)

1. Do not worry excessively about the material things of life.

2. Nobody can make their lives longer by even one minute by worrying or being anxious about it. So there is no point in doing so.

3. Seek first of all the kingdom of God. (12:31)

Almsgiving (12:33–34)

Questions (third set)

1. Good disciples of Jesus should be ready to sacrifice their possessions, give money to the poor, and concentrate on 'spiritual riches' which nobody can steal.

2. Probably surprised.

3. Members of religious orders, who take a vow of poverty, and give up the right to personal possessions, do this in an obvious way, but anyone who is ready to make sacrifices for

the poor and needy and puts following Jesus before material possessions is acting in the spirit of Jesus's teaching.

Margin Notes [p.130]

Discuss
No. Taking out insurances is sensible (and is sometimes rightly required by law, e.g. insurance for vehicles to protect the rights of everyone who might be involved in an accident). Life insurance is also a sensible safeguard especially in the case of someone who has responsibilities for providing for a family. The difference is that the former is merely a safeguard and does not suggest undue worry or concern. So far as the latter is concerned, what Jesus means is over-concern for such matters, perhaps even an unhealthy obsession which might prevent people from 'getting on with their lives' and doing with them the things that God expects from them, or which would fix their attention on material welfare and possessions at the expense of what is really important.

Where your treasure is
What people value most in life is what they will devote most of their love to. Treasure might be money, property in general, 'high living', food and drink, power. Conversely it could be their relationship with God. And, together with this it could be their families, true friendship, helping less-fortunate people.

Question [p.131]
This is probably a reference to the Messianic Banquet. Refer the pupils back to the passages which introduced this theme, to be found on pages 108, 114, 124, 128.

The Rich Man and Lazarus (16:19–31)

Questions [p.132]

1. 'There was a rich man, who was clothed in purple and fine linen and who feasted sumptuously every day.' (16:19)

2. He was ... 'full of sores, who desired to be fed with what fell from the rich man's table; moreover the dogs came and licked the sores.

3. Lazarus was in full view at his very gate.

4. Because he neglected to look after the poor, represented here by Lazarus. He could have given help to the poor and *still* had plenty for himself, but he chose not to do this!

5. Yes. An identical message. Rich nations must give aid to poorer ones. They must certainly not do the opposite (as often happens) and exploit them.

The Wealthy Ruler (18:18–23)

Question
That it entails making great sacrifices and, as we have seen earlier, it is never an easy way of life!

The Danger of Wealth (18:24–27)

Question
Because people get so attached to them and find it very difficult to let them go. Such people may give all or much of their time to looking after their wealth at the expense of their duties towards God and their neighbours.

Reward for the Disciple of Jesus 18:28–30

Questions (first set) [p.133]

1. Yes, he was a good man—he obeyed the *Torah* since he was very young (some of the more important commandments are mentioned here). However, he was very rich and his riches got in the way of his being a disciple—he was not able to give them up.

2. As we have seen in previous passages, it is not easy—especially for those attached to their possessions. Jesus said, 'it is easier for a camel to pass through the eye of a needle than for a rich man to enter the kingdom of God.' (18:25) A person cannot 'make it' by himself; he needs God's help. After Jesus's words just quoted, the disciples ask, 'Then who can be saved?' His answer was, 'What is impossible with men is possible with God.' (18:27)

3. Eternal life.

4. All who devote themselves to following Jesus, even at cost to themselves.

Parable of the Pounds 19:11–27

Questions (second set)

1. Probably Jesus. He would go to a far country (heaven) to 'receive kingly power' (from God). He would then return (the *parousia* or second coming) to judge all mankind on how they have led their lives.

2. They have made good use of the talents and gifts God has given them. They are God's property, given to people to put them to good use. They have made profitable use of their talents and so have led useful lives (perhaps attracting more people into the kingdom).

3. Because he had wasted his talents and gifts (which, remember, are God's property!) and so wasted his life and his place in the kingdom!

4. The answer is in v.27, 'But as for these enemies of mine, who did not want me to reign over them, bring them here and slay them before me.'

5. God has given everyone talents which he expects them to use for the good of the kingdom. Those who neglect to do this, for example because they have an unhealthy love for material possessions, stand in danger of losing their eternal life. Similarly with those who actively work against the kingdom by leading a sinful life, by engaging in acts of violence, for example.

Looking Back—Revision Exercises   [p.134]

1. She washed his feet and then anointed them with oil (Student Text, p.121).

2. The one who owed more was the more grateful to have his debts forgiven. Similarly with sinners. Everyone is a sinner but God is ready to forgive those who repent. It would be harder for those who are the greater sinners (e.g. the sinful woman) to repent—but such people would afterwards have the greater love for God.

3. 'And who is my neighbour?' (10:29b)

4. 'You shall love the Lord your God with all your heart, and with all your soul, and with all your strength, and with all your mind', quoted by the Lawyer in 10:27. See also p.121.

5. A Samaritan. He bound the man's wounds, pouring on oil and wine; set him on his own beast, brought him to an inn, took care of him. The next day he gave the innkeeper two denarii to look after the man until his (the Samaritan's) return, and he promised to pay any further expenses.

6. 'There will be more joy in heaven over one sinner who repents than over ninety-nine righteous persons who need no repentance.' (15:7)

7. Jesus tell us to forgive them every time. He actually says 'seven times' but this was an expression meaning 'a limitless number.' See a fuller explanation on p.123.

8. 'If you had faith as a grain of mustard seed, you could say to this sycamine tree, 'Be rooted up, and be planted in the sea,' and it would obey you' (Luke 17:6; also p.123).

9. Because Zacchaeus was a tax-collector and therefore a great sinner. For a rabbi (and a prophet!) to want to be associated with such a person was a scandal!

10. The Son of Man.

11. Because you may be asked to move to a lower one! (See Luke 14:9.)

12. People who have high opinions of themselves are often not considered great by God, and vice versa. The Pharisee felt sure that he was worthy of God's kingdom but was not, and remained unworthy. The tax-collector knew he was unworthy, but because he repented humbly, he became acceptable (p.124).

13. Mary Magdalene; Joanna, the wife of Chuza; Suzanna. (Any two!)

14. An allegory is a story in which each character or item represents or symbolises some other person, thing or group. In the allegory of the Sower the seed represents the word of God.

15. The one given on p.126. The lamp is the teaching of Jesus—it must not be hidden away but displayed for all to share. Teachers should use their professional judgement in crediting other explanations offered.

16. Mary. The 'good portion' was to sit at the feet of the Lord and listen to his teaching (10:38–42).

17. The original guests who made excuses (p.128).

18. 'Father, hallowed be thy name. Thy kingdom come. Give us each day our daily bread; and forgive us our sins, for we ourselves forgive everyone who is indebted to us: and lead us not into temptation.' (11:2b–4)

19. Like the widow in the story, people should persevere in prayer and not give up if God appears to be slow in answering. God always answers prayer. This is not an allegory—God is not an unrighteous judge!

20. Because he was relying on his material possessions for his future and these would be useless to him! Instead, he should have put his trust in the kingdom to be sure of riches that would last.

21. See p.131 of the Student Text. Jesus was expressing the wish that his disciples would work as hard concerning the kingdom of God as this man did in getting himself out of the fix he was in.

22. 'They have Moses and the prophets, let them hear them... if they do not hear Moses and the prophets, neither will they be convinced if someone should rise from the dead' (16:29,31).

23. To sell all their possessions, give the money to the poor and follow Jesus unreservedly (for example, 18:22).

24. '... manifold more in this time, and in the age to come eternal life' (18:30).

25. They can expect spiritual death—in other words to lose eternal life. It is Luke 19:27 which tells us, 'But as for these enemies of mine, who did not want me to reign over them, bring them here and slay them before me.'

UNIT 3 (Alternative B)

ISSUES IN CHRISTIAN LIVING

Section A : Fundamental Attitudes

This Section deals successively with the topics detailed in the syllabus content, and includes treatment of the texts prescribed in connection with these, as appropriate. In the outline given below, indication is given of the subsections in which *texts prescribed in the syllabus* occur.

Outline of Section A

1. *Choosing the Right Direction*
   Texts: *Mt 6:21–23*

2. *The Basic Christian Attitude—Love*
   Texts: *Lk 10:25–28*

3. *The Parable of The Good Samaritan*
   Texts: *Lk 10:29–37*

4. *God and Love*

5. *Love of God*
   Prayer and worship

6. *Love of God and Love of Neighbour*
   Texts: *1 Jn 4:7–12,20–21*

7. *Love of Neighbour—Attitude and Action*
   Texts: *1 Jn 3:11–18*

8. *Love—Foundation of the Commandments*
   Texts: *Exodus 20:1–17; Rom 13:8–10*

9. *Love is Sacrificial*
   Texts: *1 Jn 3:16*

10. *Laying Down One's Life*

11. *Humility*
    Example of Jesus, Blessed Virgin Mary
    Parable of Pharisee and Tax Collector

    SUMMARY
    Texts: *Phil 2:3–11; Lk 1:46–55; 18:9–14*

The general aim of this section is to promote understanding of the fundamental attitudes which should shape and characterize a Christian's conduct and way of life. Accordingly it is not only important in itself, but also serves as a basis for the consideration of the various topics dealt with in Section B. It introduces fundamental principles and criteria which will be employed there. It is also a kind of continuation and further exploration of ideas contained in Unit 1, Section B—especially some of those contained in subsection 7, ' Communicating Salvation' (pp.43–46). This Section, in fact, amounts to a further exploration of what is meant by a 'living faith'.

In this Section particularly, as will be observed, each subsection is quite short and usually focuses on one central point. It should be observed, however, that length of treatment is no sure indication of the actual importance of any topic or concept.

1.   *Choosing the Right Direction*   [pp.137–138]

The principal aim of this introductory subsection is to get pupils asking questions about what is *really* valuable and important and about the effects on people of the values by which they live. It is our values and principles which shape the judgements we make about how we should act. If they are wrong, the direction of our lives will be wrong. If they are right, we at least know the general direction in which we should be going. Our values indicate what we are really like, or at least what we are trying to be like. The point is made with references to the prescribed text Mt 6:21–23, which is of fundamental importance. It underlines the importance of having the right values and priorities, and of living by them.

The questions in the body of the text on p.137 and the questions on p.138 are intended to form a basis for discussion of these matters.

Additional Activity
In addition to the activity suggested in the margin of p.137, pupils might be asked to do the following exercise.

1.   List what you think are *really* the most important things in life, and give a reason for choosing each.

2. List any particular ambitions you have.

3. Is there any conflict between the two lists, or are they compatible?

4. If they ever proved to be incompatible, which do you think should come first?

They might also be asked to consider privately whether or not they actually lived as though the things they had listed in answer to question 1 were really the most important.

2. *The Basic Christian Attitude — Love* [p.139]

This subsection clearly goes closely with subsection 3. Both are based on one or other parts of the prescribed text (Lk 10:25–37). It is treated typographically as a distinct subsection (albeit a brief one) because it serves as a kind of prologue not only to subsection 3, but to much of the rest of the Section as well, especially subsections 4–7. It also makes a very important point, which might easily be passed over if presented as merely an introduction to the parable of the Good Samaritan. That point is that the *first* commandment concerns *love of God*. For both these reasons, which are inter-connected, the material in this subsection is of fundamental importance, and deserves emphasis.

The nature of love is discussed later in this Unit and also in Unit 5.

3. *Parable of the Good Samaritan* [p.140]

The main point of the parable is that it is meant to provide the answer to the question 'Who is my neighbour?' and therefore, effectively, 'Who must I love as myself?' The interpretation given at the end of p.140 is meant as a basis for discussion.

Questions

1. A number of points may be made. For example, neither virtue nor lack of virtue is always to be found where it might be expected. Also, one cannot determine the virtue or character of anyone simply on the basis of race, nationality or

religion, or indeed on the basis of social position and
respectability (or lack of it).

2.   See text.

3.   To show how much trouble and care the Samaritan took in
      helping the man. It was not just a token gesture or a
      half-hearted effort. He really put himself out.

4.   Compassion.

Something to Do
Obviously the modern 'Samaritan' would have to be one of a
despised group. It might be a group generally held in low esteem,
or one held in low esteem in certain circles. It might also be
interesting to discuss who might qualify as a 'Samaritan' in the
eyes of a variety of different groups.

4.   *God and Love*   [p.141]

This subsection, though brief, is important. It offers a basis for the
value ascribed to love by Christians, and lays the foundation for
the notion of God as the *source* of all real love. In particular, it
accounts for the fact that it is the command to love which is the
basic Christian commandment. It is not an arbitrary command, but
one based on God himself and on the destiny he offers human
beings. The last sentence on p.141 contains a key idea. 'We must
be like him, it we want to live with him'.

Background Note
The notion of God as *love itself* is closely connected with, and
made more intelligible by, the doctrine of the Trinity. Love always
requires an object. It is always love *of* something or someone (even
if only oneself). Its highest expression is as a relationship of
self-giving between *persons*. It is the doctrine of the Trinity which
enables us to see how God can *be* perfect love in an absolute sense.
The one God is not simply a solitary being, but actually an
inter-relationship of Persons, bound together in perfect unity—
unity of being and unity in love. All that the Son has (the whole
being of God) he receives eternally from the Father. All that the
Spirit has he receives eternally from the Father and the Son (or

through the Son). All are bound together in a perfect union of being, life and love.

Human self-giving, however profound, is in itself limited and incomplete, but in God it is unlimited and total. God is the uniquely perfect communion of self-giving personal love, in which what each possesses is possessed by all. All love tends towards union. In God alone is that union complete and perfect. All true love is not only a reflection of the love that God *is*, but is a gift that comes to us from him, who is the source of all love.

5. *Love of God* [pp.142–3]

This subsection begins consideration of the first great commandment—concerning love of God. Its principal aim is to promote understanding of prayer and worship as means of expressing and fostering such love. It is not intended as a general review and examination of prayer.

Key points
- Prayer and worship are involved in love of God, because love is concerned with union, and it is through prayer and worship that union with God is promoted.
- For Catholics, the Eucharist is *the* way of deepening union with God through Jesus Christ:
  - because it is a participation in Jesus's perfect offering of himself to the Father;
  - because in Holy Communion they believe that they receive Jesus Christ himself, who comes to unite them more closely with him as children of God. (This is more fully dealt with in Unit 4, but should be introduced here.)
- Corporate prayer and worship are important because we relate to God not just as individuals, but as members of a community (a family). Loving God involves living and praying as part of his family, and not just as isolated individuals.

Prayer
The principal aim of the activity suggested in the margin of p.142

is to ensure that pupils have a sufficiently broad understanding of the nature of prayer, and do not regard it as simply intercession.

6. *Love of God and Love of Neighbour* [pp.144–5]

This completes the treatment of the love of God, begun in the previous subsection. It focuses on two passages from the First Letter of St John (both prescribed texts). The principal aim is to promote understanding of the connection between love of God and love of neighbour, as required by the syllabus.

The key point is that all real love comes from God, and is indivisible. It is the same love which enables us to love God and to love our neighbour. This means that, if we do not love our neighbour, we cannot have God's gift of love within us, and therefore cannot truly love God. To love God involves loving what he loves. God loves everyone. Therefore loving one's neighbour is part of what is meant by loving God. To have God's love in our hearts means loving others, because God's love is for everyone.

Questions [p.144]

1. Because love is 'of God'.

2. Because 'God is love'.

3. Because he sent his Son into the world 'to be the expiation for our sins'.

4. One answer is: because we should want to be like God.

7. *Love of Neighbour — Attitude and Action* [pp.146–7]

This subsection now deals further with the nature and characteristics of love of neighbour. It centres on two prescribed texts: 1 Jn 3:1–18, Jas 2:14–17. The principal aim is to encourage understanding of love of neighbour as a lived attitude, with practical effects, rather than simply emotion or good intentions.

Questions [p.146]

1. Murder.

2. See Gen 4:1–11.

3.   (a) He is not living with the life of God.

     (b) He is a murderer in his heart. He has the same attitude as a murderer to his victim.

4.   The fact that Jesus laid down his life for us.

5.   Something like: Let us show our love in how we act, and not just talk about it.

Margin Note: 'Hate the sin, but love the sinner'   [p.146]
Pupils may have some difficulty with this. The point, of course, is that one is commanded to love everyone, even enemies and those who do one harm, but that does not mean that one is supposed to approve of their evil deeds. Conversely, one should hate sin, as God does, because it is evil and contrary to goodness and love, but one should have care and concern for those who do evil, just as God has. The distinction becomes easier to understand, once it is realised that 'love' in this sense does not necessarily imply liking or approval or affection. We can still love people whose character and personalities we find distasteful or repulsive.

8. *Love — Foundation of the Commandments*   [pp.148–149]

The principal aim is to promote acquaintance with the Ten Commandments and an understanding of their relationship to the fundamental law of love.

The Ten Commandments
The version given on p.148 is that found in Exodus 20:2–17 (a prescribed text). The note in the margin gives the form of Commandments 9 and 10 (based on the version in Deuteronomy) which is traditionally used by Catholics.

[p.149]   Pupils are asked to explain how the acts forbidden in Commandments 4–10 offend against love of neighbour. The connection of the first three commandments with the command to love God with all one's being has already been mentioned on p.142.

It should be explained to pupils that the 'ten commandments' are not an exhaustive list of sins, but a summary, in headline form, of the principal serious offences. Traditionally in Catholic teaching they have been used as headings under which a cluster of related offences were dealt with. So, for example, under the Fifth Commandment 'You shall not kill', one can deal not only with murder, but with all kinds of unlawful violence. Under the Eighth Commandment 'You shall not bear false witness against your neighbour', one can deal with all forms of lying and all forms of harming one's neighbour by what one says. A traditional extended treatment of the Commandments, on this pattern, may be found in the *Catechism of the Catholic Church*, nos. 2083–2550.

'You shall not covet'

The Ninth and Tenth Commandments may need a little explanation. Covetousness refers to jealousy, envy, greed for what is another's. In itself the Tenth Commandment forbids the desire to deprive others of their goods, the desire to gain personal advantage unjustly at another's expense. More generally it can be extended to cover all kinds of avarice and immoderate desire for material goods.

The Ninth Commandment, 'you shall not covet your neighbour's wife' of course applies the other way round also: 'you shall not covet your neighbour's husband.' In itself it is directly concerned with illicit desires and intentions in respect of another person's spouse, but more generally it can be extended to cover all kinds of illicit sexual thoughts and desires.

Both these commandments are primarily concerned with thoughts and attitudes, They indicate that sin is a matter of mind and the heart and not merely of external acts. To wish or desire evil is itself sinful, even if it does not give rise to action.

[p.149]   This subsection concludes with the important point which should be emphasised, that though the law of love includes the Commandments, it goes beyond them. The Commandments tell us primarily what is *not* in accordance with love. The law of love itself requires us not only to avoid certain things, but also actively to do good.

9. Love is Sacrificial [p.150]

This and the following subsection complete the treatment of the nature of love given in this Unit. They contain points of fundamental importance. The key notions are that:

- real love is not merely emotion or nice feelings;
- it is not merely attraction;
- it is essentially *self-giving*.

The great example is Jesus.

Additional Activities and Exercises
In addition to the question in the margin of p.150, pupils may be asked to suggest and discuss examples of 'real love' in action, and also other kinds of 'love'.

- What images of 'love' are given by magazines, pop songs, TV, etc?
- What do you think of them?
- Who has shown you love in your life?
- How important has that been to you?
- Make a collage illustrating the various ways in which 'love' is portrayed.

10. Laying Down One's Life [pp.151–2]

This continues to explore the kind of 'sacrifices' real love may entail: from actual martyrdom to more mundane examples. The aim is to promote appreciation of the demanding nature of real love and of the courage it requires, and also to encourage pupils to determine whether there is need for more courage in their own lives.

Additional Activity
Pupils might be asked to give examples (real or imaginary) of the kind of situations mentioned on p.152, and to say in each case what might cause people not to do the right thing.

Knowing and Doing
The last paragraph on p.152 mentions the necessity of God's help, and the consequent importance of prayer and the Sacraments. This

raises an important point, and one which should be discussed with pupils. At the beginning of this Section, the questions was raised as to what principles or attitudes should govern our life and guide our judgements. Love is given as the basic Christian answer. It is important to realise, however, that while the *law of love* may furnish a general guide which can help us to judge what kind of things we *should* do and what we *should* avoid, that in itself does not ensure that we will actually follow such judgements. Many people know full well what they should and should not do, but that knowledge does not in itself cause them to behave as they should. For that, what is needed is not just the law of love, but the *gift of love* itself. It is that which makes us able to do what we know the law of love requires. It is a gift which comes from God, and which we can allow to grow stronger within us through prayer and the Sacraments.

11. *Humility* [pp.153–6]

The aim is to clarify the nature and importance of the Christian idea of humility, and to distinguish it from attitudes with which it might be confused. The treatment centres on three prescribed texts. One of these (Phil 2:3–11) will already be familiar from Unit 1. The second is the text of the *Magnificat* (Lk 1:46–55). In these, Jesus and Mary successively are presented as models of humility. The third is the parable of the Pharisee and the Tax-Collector (Lk 18:9–14). All of these should be thoroughly discussed. The pupils' initial characterization of 'humility' (Exercise on p.153) should be discussed in class as a preliminary, and both positive and negative features noted.

Questions [p.154]

1. 'My soul magnifies the Lord, and my spirit rejoices in God my Saviour.'
    'He has regarded the low estate of his handmaiden.'
    'He that is mighty has done great things for me, and holy is his name.'

2. Those of 'low degree', the hungry.

3. Joyful, thankful, exultant.

Additional Exercise

Pupils could be asked to discuss and answer the following questions:

- Can you think of a well-known person (or a character on TV) who you think is 'humble', and one you think is 'proud'?
- What do you think of each?
- Do you think you have humility? If so, in what way?
- In what ways, if any, do you think you lack humility?

Additional Notes

The photograph on p.156 is of Mother Teresa of Calcutta and two other members of her Congregation: the 'Missionaries of Charity'.

The SUMMARY (p.156) may be found useful as a basis for revision.

Section B

Negative and Positive implications of Love

This Section deals successively with the topics detailed in the syllabus content, and includes treatment of the texts prescribed in connection with these, as appropriate. In the outline given below, indication is given of the subsection in which texts *prescribed in the syllabus* occur.

Outline of Section B

1. *Individual and Social*

2. *Justice*
   Dishonesty: in word—in deed
   Violence
   Unjust Discrimination
   Social Justice
   Scraps from the Rich Man's Table
   Texts: *Jas 2:1–4, Is 58:6–10. Amos 8:4–7, Lk 16:19–31, Mt 25:31–46*

3. *Mercy*
   Mercy and forgiveness
   Forgiveness and reconciliation
   The Sacrament of Reconciliation
   Texts: *Mt 5:43–48, 18:21–35*

4. *Use and Abuse of Gifts*
   Parable of the Talents
   Misuse of gifts
   Stewards of the world
   Abuse of drugs and alcohol
   Texts: *Mt 25:14–30, Lk 12:13–31, Gen 1:26–31*

Preliminary Background Notes

The following notes are not meant to form the basis of a specific lesson to be given to pupils. They are meant as a guide to teachers concerning some of the principles which should be employed in discussing moral judgements from a Catholic perspective. The substance of points made here may be introduced at appropriate places in this and other Units (especially Unit 5). It is hoped that this summary treatment may be found useful by teachers as a point of reference.

In Part B of this Unit and elsewhere in the course pupils are often asked to consider the *consequences* of certain actions, attitudes etc. This procedure serves to draw attention to one important aspect which has a bearing on the morality of acts. The person seeking to live a moral life must seek to live responsibly, and this involves taking account of the possible or likely consequences of his/her behaviour. It is moreover true that evil conduct commonly gives rise, directly or indirectly, to much consequent evil both for individuals and society at large, and it is as well for pupils to become aware of this. At the same time, as the following notes make clear, one cannot assess the morality of an act *simply* on an estimation of its likely consequences or on whether those consequences involve more or less good than evil in any given situation. Other factors, and in the first place the nature of the act in itself, have to be taken into account.

A moral act is one which is consistent with love of God above all things and love of neighbour as oneself. It is an act which is in accordance with the dignity of human beings, made in the image and likeness of God, and called to eternal life with him. According to Catholic teaching, nothing which contradicts the law of God can, objectively speaking, be considered morally good, and therefore in accordance with the true demands of love or conducive to the real good of the human person. This law in its principal features is accessible to reason, but is further clarified and illuminated by revelation and the light of faith.

A. MORAL ACTS

Introduction

In Catholic moral teaching, three components are traditionally mentioned, when judging the rightness or wrongness of an act: the act itself, the intention and the circumstances (especially likely consequences).

The Act in Itself

Consideration of the act itself is of prime importance. It must not in itself be wrong. If it is, it cannot be made good by either good intentions or good consequences. One may not do evil, so that good may come about, or to put it another way, *the end does not justify the means.*

A good intention may make a bad act less evil than it might otherwise be, but it does not make it good or justifiable. So, for example, to steal in order to give money to charity is clearly better than to steal for one's own selfish purposes, but is still wrong.

It is right to want to persuade a firm to end unjust treatment of its employees, and the consequences of doing so successfully may be considered good, but it is still wrong to do so by setting fire to one of the firm's warehouses or by threatening the lives of the managing director's family. If someone in authority is unfairly making the lives of his subordinates a misery, it is right to want to change this, and the beneficial consequences of doing so may be great, but it is still wrong to secure his removal by falsely accusing him of a criminal offence.

Intention

When an act is not in itself wrong, intention and circumstances are particularly important. A bad intention will make bad an act which outwardly may appear good. So, for example, visiting a lonely old man is not in itself wrong and if it is done with the intention of befriending him and helping him to feel less lonely, it is positively good. If, however, it is done in order to find out where he keeps his money, so that one may steal from him, then it is clearly hypocritical and wrong. In general, when the act is not in itself wrong, the better the intention, the better the act.

Circumstances

One must, however, take account of the circumstances in which the act is performed, especially in respect of its foreseeable likely consequences. In circumstances where an act which is not itself wrong would have foreseeable consequence/dangers which cannot be properly justified, it would be wrong to perform it. For example, for an experienced driver to drive very fast on a race track is one thing; for anyone to do so on a busy public highway is another. Similarly, to give a box of matches to a five year old is very different from giving one to an adult. In considering how one should act, the duty of loving one's neighbour as oneself always obliges one to take seriously the consequences of one's actions.

The Principle of Double Effect

Often, however, acts may have both good and bad consequences. If one could never do anything which carried the risk of any bad consequence, life would be virtually impossible, and much good could not be achieved. This problem is addressed by what is known as the principle of double effect. This states that:

(a) the act itself must not be wrong;

(b) the good effect must not itself be the direct consequence of the bad effect;

(c) the bad effect must not be directly intended, even if foreseen, i.e. it must be an undesired by-product of the action;

(d) there must be a proportionately grave reason to justify permitting the risk or probability of the bad effect. (Especially in serious cases, there would have to be no safer practicable alternative, and all reasonable practicable precautions would have to be taken to minimize the risk.)

The exact gravity of the reason required will depend upon the gravity of the anticipated possible evil effect and on its degree of probability. A very grave reason is required for a course of action which entails a probable serious risk to human life.

Examples

To take an everyday example; a parent has a duty to preserve his/her small child from harm. He/she anticipates that allowing the child to play with some boisterous neighbouring children may well be of benefit to the child, but will also quite likely involve the probability of some minor injuries. Providing that all reasonable precautions are taken and that there is adequate supervision, it would be unreasonable to prevent the child playing simply for this reason. The necessity for the child to develop normally and to enjoy the company of other children provides a perfectly adequate reason for tolerating this slight degree of risk. On the other hand, if the children were planning to go and play on the railway line, that would be another matter. There is a difference between what is prudent and reasonable and what is reckless and foolish.

Here is another example. A government has to decide whether to initiate a nation-wide vaccination of children against whooping cough. It knows that vaccination will be effective in the vast majority of cases, that it will save many children's lives and preserve many others from serious harm. It also knows that it is statistically highly likely that a comparatively small number of children will be made very ill by the vaccine, and that some will die. The likelihood of this for any child is very small, but the possibility is still there. Let us judge this case by the principle of double effect.

(a) Vaccination is not in itself wrong.
(b) The good effect is not the direct consequence of the bad; the children who are saved are not saved *because* of the deaths of the others. They would be saved whether any other children died or not.
(c) The bad effect is not directly intended. It is not the aim of the vaccination programme to kill children. Any deaths are neither intended nor desired.
(d) The fact that more children will die or be seriously

harmed, if there is no vaccination programme, than will die or be seriously harmed if there is, appears to provide a proportionately grave reason for tolerating the risk of the bad effect.

In the same way, any parent who has to decide whether the risk of vaccination is justifiable can reason quite rightly that it is in fact more risky for the child not to be vaccinated than otherwise, Therefore the decision to vaccinate is a perfectly responsible and morally justifiable decision. Of course, if there were some way of determining safely in advance whether the child would respond badly to the vaccine, that should be tried, but if there were, there would be no problem.

B. CONSCIENCE

Moral conscience is a judgment of reason by which a person perceives the moral quality of an act—what he/she should do or not do in particular cases. It is a judgment made through the use of reason, illumined by revelation and the light of faith, and guided by the authoritative teaching of the Church. It is not simply a matter of 'gut-feeling' or the emotion of the moment. It is the means by which each judges how best to comply with the fundamental divine law inscribed on his/her heart; to do good and avoid evil. The voice of conscience has an imperative quality; it speaks of what we 'must' or 'ought to' do or avoid. It passes judgment on the choices we actually make, approving some, denouncing others.

According to Catholic teaching, a person must always follow the dictates of his/her conscience. This is the case even if one's conscience is in fact erroneous, as long as the person is truly acting in good faith. The action itself would still objectively be wrong, but the person concerned would be free from blame. Each person, however, has a duty to inform his/her conscience properly, and to exercise due care in reaching moral judgments, especially in serious matters. People whose erroneous conscience is the result of inadequate concern for what is true and good or whose conscience has been dulled by habits of sin are not without blame, and in some cases may be seriously blameworthy. Catholics are considered to have a duty to attend to and be guided by the authoritative teaching of the Church.

C. CULPABILITY

Closely connected with what has been said above is the question of culpability, i.e. blameworthiness. In Catholic moral teaching, culpability presumes some degree of knowledge, deliberation and consent.

Knowledge

The person must have some realisation that what he/she is doing is wrong. To be guilty of a grave sin requires realisation that the offence is serious. If, for some reason, someone committed an offence which was objectively wrong, but in good faith believed that it was a good act, he would not be accounted blameworthy.

Deliberation

The person must have performed the act deliberately, realising what he was doing, i.e. not accidentally or without thinking what he was doing. Lack of full deliberation can lessen the degree of culpability, and may make what would have been a grave sin into a slighter offence.

Consent

The person must have consented freely to the act. Anything which limits freedom may lessen culpability, e.g. fear, coercion. However, particularly in really serious matters, the mere fact of fear or coercion does not in itself mean that the person is not still guilty of grave sin. It all depends to what extent fear actually does take away someone's capacity to act freely. Someone who is so overcome by fear, fatigue, pain or emotion that he is literally no longer responsible for his actions may in fact be free from serious blame, but not everyone who experiences even serious fear, fatigue, etc. is actually in that situation. The decisive factor is not so much the degree of coercion etc. which is inflicted as the actual resultant capacity to resist evil and do good. Insanity or severe mental disturbance will normally render a person incapable of the degree of free consent necessary for serious sin.

The Scope and Emphases of this Section
This Section looks at a range of issues in a fairly concise and outline manner. The treatment in the Student Text is mainly concerned to promote awareness of the principles and moral/religious factors involved, rather than with providing detailed information about specific concrete cases or about the work of relevant agencies. It is, however, advantageous for pupils to look at actual specified examples in the areas covered by this Section, and teachers are well advised to provide some for them. Topical examples may often be the best, and the fact that topicality is a transient quality is one reason why actual cases are not introduced in the Student Text. Newspapers, magazines, TV programmes etc. may all be profitably used in this regard (sometimes as an object for criticism). There are also a number of agencies involved in appropriate fields which will provide information both about their own work and concerning relevant issues and cases. Attention is drawn to some of these at various points in the notes on this Section.

Having said that, it remains important to remember that pupils are to be examined chiefly on their knowledge and understanding of the principles, and moral and religious factors involved in dealing with questions in these areas, and on their capacity to comment effectively on them. While some outline knowledge of specific contemporary cases may be useful, a concentration on simply amassing a wealth of empirical data would be mistaken, and would detract from the main emphasis of the Section.

It is a common complaint among examiners of Religious Studies syllabuses that, in these areas, the answers of candidates are often unsatisfactory, because they focus too heavily on the provision of empirical data and tend to adopt a simply descriptive or pragmatic approach, with little, if any, advertence to the religious, spiritual and moral dimensions with which the syllabus is primarily concerned. It must be remembered that this is specifically a Religious Studies (rather than simply a Social Studies) syllabus. The emphasis must be on the relevance and implications of specific religious beliefs, moral values and principles for attitudes and conduct in the areas under discussion.

1. *Individual and Social* [p.157]

The aim of this introductory paragraph is to draw attention to the social dimension of moral questions. In discussing moral issues, there is a danger of focusing too exclusively either on the individual or on society at large. One can indeed come across individuals who are much concerned about social issues, but who in the conduct of their personal lives are vindictive, malicious, untruthful and dishonest, who profess a concern for the human race as a whole or for human 'problems' in the abstract, which is at variance with their attitudes and actions towards the individual human beings they come into contact with. On the other hand, one may also come across people who are scrupulously honest and upright in the conduct of their personal lives, but who evince little concern for or interest in general questions of social justice.

In this section an attempt is made to strike an appropriate balance. When matters of individual conduct are dealt with, an attempt is generally made to introduce discussion of the wider social effects of individual wrongdoing etc., and when the issue is primarily of a wider social nature, attention is generally drawn to the implications they hold for the attitudes and conduct of individuals.

2. *Justice* [pp.157–171]

This subsection makes no attempt at a thorough analysis of the concept of Justice (or of its divisions). It takes simply a very general idea of the concept, as a working definition, and then proceeds to consider various ways in which what is due to others can be denied or delivered.

[p.157]   The question at the bottom of the left-hand column (concerning 'rights') is meant only to alert pupils to the distinction between what may be desirable and what is strictly a 'right'. There may well be disagreement as to where the boundaries should be drawn. Too much time should not be spent on matters of detail. It would be useful, however, to introduce the idea that some rights are fundamental and inalienable, while others are much more subject to qualification and to legitimate regulation for the common good. For example, the right to private property is a true right, but public authorities have the right to regulate its exercise for the common good. The point should be made that an individual's exercise of his own rights must always be regulated by a concern not to infringe the rights of others, and that rights imply corresponding duties.

The following list of rights, found in the Decree of the Second Vatican Council on 'The Church In The Modern World' (*Gaudium et Spes*) may be found useful as a basis for discussion.

> '... ready access to all that is necessary for living a genuinely human life; for example, food, clothing, housing, the right freely to choose his state in life and set up a family, the right to education, work, to his good name, to respect, to proper knowledge, the right to act according to the dictates of conscience and to safeguard his privacy, and rightful freedom even in matters of religion.' (*Gaudium et Spes 26*).

Note the general characterization of all these as: 'all that is necessary for living a genuinely human life'. Many things which may be desirable are not strictly 'necessary' for this purpose.

The principal aims of this whole, rather long sub-section are to promote awareness of concern for justice:
- as a fundamental implication of 'love of neighbour';
- as an attitude with implications for many areas and aspects of life.

Injustice implies a lack of concern for the rights and welfare of others, and a corresponding selfish exaltation of one's own interests at the expense of others; it exposes attitudes directly contrary to 'love of neighbour'. It is with the aim of bringing out this point that, from time to time, pupils are asked what a certain kind of behaviour tells one about the attitude of the perpetrator (a) to others, (b) to himself.

Truth — Background Notes
The value of truth finds its basis in God himself. Christ himself is proclaimed as 'the Truth' and therefore truthfulness and fidelity are important aspects of authentic Christian living. They reflect:

- the fidelity of God to his promises
- the fidelity of Christ to his Father and to his mission.

The trustworthiness of God and of his Son, Jesus Christ, needs to be reflected in the lives and conduct of Christians. Regard for truth has therefore a theological foundation. In any case, trust is an essential pre-requisite for harmonious social living which will protect and foster the rights and well-being of people, and trust requires a respect for the demands of truth and fidelity. Truth is necessary to enable people to make right choices, to collaborate with each other, to achieve their purposes and to find and fulfil meaning in life. There is therefore a *natural right* to truth and a corresponding duty of truthfulness.

This right is not, however, absolute. It does not imply that anyone has an automatic right to know everything about everyone, nor that one must always disclose everything. There is also a right to privacy, a right to one's good name, and duties to protect legitimate secrets and to preserve confidences which mean that one is not bound always to reveal the whole truth. Indeed, there are occasions when one has a duty not to reveal some of the truth. Unless there are compelling reasons, one should not ordinarily retail discreditable information about others, even if true. Only if a higher duty (e.g. to protect others from serious harm) requires it, should one reveal what one has been told in confidence.

Ordinarily this causes little difficulty. One simply does not speak about such matters. If one meets with intrusive questioning (e.g. about the private life of oneself or one's family, or about a confidential matter which one has a duty not to reveal) or indeed about any matter which the questioner has no *right* to know, one can simply be non-committal or change the subject or refuse to discuss the matter, or tell the person to mind his own business. In circumstances where such expedients would not work, and when one has a sufficient reason for not giving the information required, moral writers generally concede that one may say something which is not in itself untrue, but which is likely to mislead. A famous example is that of St John Chrysostom fleeing from unjust persecution. The agents who were pursuing him along a river actually caught up with him, but not recognising him in the gloom, asked him whether he had seen John Chrysostom. 'Oh yes', he said, 'He's not far away. You've almost got him.' The agents thanked him, and sped off up the river.

The Catholic moral tradition has maintained a general prohibition on telling lies (i.e. knowingly saying what is *untrue* in order to deceive). The question has been raised as to whether there are any circumstances in which telling a falsehood might be justifiable, and some have argued that, especially when there are serious moral reasons why certain information should not be disclosed, and other means are likely to be ineffective, then it may be permissible. One way of justifying this would be to say, in effect, that a 'real' lie is telling an untruth with an unjustifiable intention of deceiving to *someone who has a right to know.* According to such an argument, where the person concerned has no right to know, and especially where one has a duty in justice or charity not to tell him, one may tell a falsehood without it being a 'real' lie.

It is fair to say that this opinion is somewhat controversial. However, the *Catechism of the Catholic Church* states: 'To lie is to speak or act against the truth in order to lead into error *someone who has the right to know the truth*' (2483). Though this does not refer to or necessarily endorse the position set out above, it does not seem to be incompatible with it. In any case, whatever is said in respect of exceptional circumstances, the great value and importance of truth require that great respect be given to the general prohibition of 'speaking a falsehood with the intention of deceiving'. Christians should be truthful people, with a great regard for the truth and an aversion to lying.

Dishonesty in Deed

Discuss [p.158]
Other examples of forms of theft could be added by the teacher. In

all cases, they involve depriving (wholly or in part) others of what is rightly theirs. That is why they are unjust.

Situation A [p.159]

1. The principal reason for the comments in parentheses is to lead pupils to consider the matter from the perspective of 'the golden rule'. They help to get over the point that an action of this kind is not just accepting 'good luck', but involves lack of concern for the interests of others.

2. It should not. The find provides enough information to make positive identification of the real owner perfectly feasible. But it might emphasize what the right course of action is, and make it easier.

3. The fact that his holiday was at the expense of another's misfortune, which he might have remedied, and which, for all he knew, might have caused the other person serious difficulties. The fact that he was a thief.

4. Lack of concern for others.

Situation B

The basic argument is that they have no right to take what belongs to another. Good intentions do not make right what is wrong. There are also the consequences for shopowners in terms of loss of income and the necessity for security measures, and consequences for other customers in terms of higher prices. In general, they are contributing to building up in society a mood of suspicion and lack of trust. If they were shopkeepers, would they think it all right, if somebody stole from them?

Non-Physical Violence [p.161]

This may provide an opportunity to discuss non-physical forms of bullying.

Unjust Discrimination

The extract from the Letter of James (p.161) is a prescribed text.

Unjust discrimination springs from the prejudiced attitude which disparages the human dignity of those it is directed against, which shows lack of concern for them, and which is hostile to their welfare. The Student Text attempts to distinguish it from legitimate forms of discrimination, which do not spring from such attitudes and which do not in themselves perpetrate injustice. One may add the following examples.

Various groupings, associations, institutions etc. will quite reasonably restrict their benefits to their members. Thus, a school will provide education for its own pupils, but not for someone who just walks in from the street, and people who live in Russia do not suffer an injustice because they are not eligible to vote in American elections. People who do not belong to certain institutions, associations, nations etc. cannot rightly complain if they do not receive from them the particular benefits reserved for those who do.

Nor is it intrinsically unjust to have associations whose membership is restricted to those who meet certain criteria. A man who owns no land and has no connection with Scotland cannot rightly complain if he is refused membership of the Scottish Landowners Association. It is unreasonable for an old-age pensioner to demand membership of the local youth club, or for a teenager to complain if he is not allowed to join the local Over Fifties club. There is nothing unjust about having clubs or associations exclusively for men or women.

Associations which are based on certain beliefs and values are perfectly entitled to admit only those who share those beliefs and values. It would be ridiculous to expect an association of total abstainers to accept as a member someone who spent every evening drinking whisky in the pub. Churches and other religious communities are also clearly doing nothing unjust in accepting only those who are prepared to share their beliefs and practices.

Discrimination is unjust when in actual fact, whatever pretext is given, the real reason is irrational prejudice, or when it involves the denial or unreasonable restriction of a person's access to something to which he/she has a right, e.g. housing, employment. One says 'unreasonable restriction' because it is not unreasonable to refuse to accept someone with a long criminal record for employment as a police officer, or someone with a record of child-abuse as a child-care worker, or someone with a record of embezzlement in a position of financial responsibility.

Racial discrimination is particularly highlighted in the Student Text, both because of its potentially disastrous consequences, and because it illustrates particularly well the true nature of unjust discrimination. It stems very obviously from an attitude which denigrates those of another race, colour etc. simply on that basis, and consequently implies an attitude which reflects adversely on their human dignity, and which is in itself irrational. Its practice moreover produces serious disadvantages for those at whom it is directed, and interferes with their legitimate access to public goods to which they have a right. It is an affront to the command to love one's neighbour as oneself.

Additional Activities
Teachers may care to broaden the perspective through one or other of the following:

- Have you ever suffered from what you thought was unjust discrimination of any kind? What form did it take? How did you feel?

- In some countries certain groups may be the object of constant violent persecution, such as, for example, homeless children on the streets of some South American cities. Find out about them and make a display.

- Throughout the world there are people who are unjustly persecuted for their religious or political views. There is a society called AMNESTY which tries to help them. Find out about it, and make a display about its work.

Social Justice   [pp.165–168]

The Scriptural passages (Is 58:6–10, Amos 8:4–7 both on p.165; Lk 16:19–31 on p.167; Mt 25:31–46 on p.168) are all prescribed texts.

Questions   [p.165]

1. Hunger, homelessness, lack of clothing.

2. Share food with the hungry, shelter the homeless, clothe the naked etc.

Questions [p.166]

1. They ask 'When will the new moon be over, that we may sell grain? And the sabbath that we may offer wheat for sale?'

2. Fraudulent tampering with weights and measures.

3. They use false balances (scales).

4. '... that we may buy the poor for silver, and the needy for a pair of sandals'. They treat the poor as commodities.

5. 'Shall not the land tremble on this account etc.'

6. 'Surely I will never forget any of their deeds'.

7. Material gain.

Questions [p.167]

1. He was clothed in purple and fine linen and feasted sumptuously every day.

2. He was full of sores, and desired to eat what fell from the rich man's table.

3. Lazarus was 'at his gate'.

4. Because he did not use his riches to help the poor.

5. See especially the passage of Isaiah on p.165, also question 2 on that page. An obvious passage from the Pentateuch is 'You shall love your neighbour as yourself'.

6. They should use their riches unselfishly and come to the help of the poor.

7. Everyone should be concerned for those in need.

Questions [p.168]

1. 'Truly as you did it to one of the least of these, my brethren, you did it to me'.

2. Concern with feeding the hungry, sheltering the homeless, clothing the naked, generally helping those in need, as part of one's duty to God.

SVP
There may well be a branch in a local parish which could help.
Information may also be obtained from: Society of St Vincent de
Paul, Damascus House, Ridgeway, London NW7 1EL (tel. 0181
906 1339).

CHAS
189a Old Brompton Road, London, SW5 0AR (tel. 0171 373
4961).

Bourne Trust
Same address as for CHAS (tel. 0171 370 6612)

There are a number of publications about the work of Mother
Teresa and her Missionaries of Charity e.g. (one of the earliest)
Malcolm Muggeridge, *Something Beautiful for God.* There is also
an organisation called 'Co-workers of Mother Teresa' who may be
able to provide information, speakers etc. The address of the local
branch will probably be found in the *Catholic Diocesan Directory*.

Information about some of the organisations mentioned in this
subsection and about some of the issues they are concerned with
may be found in 'Q Source' (See General Introduction).

Scraps from The Rich Man's Table [pp.169–171]
The Student Text gives only an outline survey of the issues.
Information about relevant organisations, and the needs of
developing countries generally may be found in 'Q Source' (see
General Introduction). CAFOD will supply information about its
own work and about relevant issues. It has a catalogue of
publications, some of them especially suitable for schools.

Addresses
• CAFOD, Romero Close, Stockwell Road, London, SW9 9TY
  (tel. 0171 733 7900).
• Aid to the Church in Need, 124 Carshalton Road, Sutton,
  Surrey, SM1 4RL

Famine
It is worth noting that the principal causes of famine are drought or

civil war or a combination of the two. Famines are not in fact caused by increases in population. Most of the famines in recent years have been in areas with low population densities. Rwanda was something of an exception in this regard, but it is abundantly clear that the famine which took place there was in no way due to the level of population, but to a cruel civil war. The ravages that such a war can cause even in a European country have been made clear by recent happenings in the former Yugoslavia.

A critical and provocative view of the 'population problem' and its alleged dangers is provided by two videos: *Facing Facts on Population*, and *The Great Population Hoax*. Both are obtainable from: Family Education Trust, 322 Woodstock Road, Oxford, OX2 7NS (tel. 01865 56848). A book on the same subject is: *The War Against Population* by Jacqueline Kasun (Ignatius Press 1988).

3. Mercy [pp.172–177]

The principal aims are:
- to emphasize that the command to love one's neighbour embraces more than simply strict justice;
- to emphasize the place of mercy and forgiveness in the Christian life;
- to promote understanding of the Sacrament of Reconciliation.

The Importance of Mercy
It is important to recognise that the command to love one's neighbour extends beyond observing the requirements of justice. Giving people what is due to them in justice is fundamentally important, but by itself it can be somewhat cold and stern. The 'golden rule', which tells us to do to others as we would have them do to us, is a good guide here. We all want people to help us when we are in difficulty, even when our basic human rights are not in question; we all want people to show us understanding and kindness, to put up with us when we are being awkward, to be patient with us, to show compassion when we are sad, and forgiveness when we need it. That is how we should treat others, and not be content with simply calculating what is due to them by

right, or with simply avoiding doing them an injustice. We need generosity of spirit.

Forgiveness
The duty of forgiveness is often stressed in the Gospels. We must forgive because God is forgiving, and we are called to be like him.

Both the texts on pp.172–73 are prescribed texts.

Questions   [p.174]

1.   God

2.   Because God is always willing to forgive us, no matter how great the offence. [By making the debt which the servant owes his master so huge, Jesus is stressing God's willingness to forgive any sin, however great.]

3.   Through the punishment given to the wicked servant.

Forgiveness and Reconciliation   [p.174]
An important point is made here. Reconciliation is necessarily something mutual, and this means that, though one should always forgive, that alone does not automatically bring about reconciliation. The case is the same with God and human beings. God's forgiveness is always there, on offer. What is often lacking is acceptance of it through repentance. Only when that is present is reconciliation (restoration of friendship) brought about for the individual.

The Meaning of Forgiveness   [pp.174–5]
The purpose of these paragraphs is to clarify the notion of forgiveness and to separate it from any *necessary* connection with emotions or 'feelings'. The point is that one need not be the slave of one's emotions, nor imagine that one is unable to forgive, simply because negative feelings remain. Of course, it is in many ways better and easier if forgiveness is accompanied by appropriate emotions, but this may not always be the case. Essentially it is a matter of attitude and will, which we can exercise much more readily that we can manufacture emotions. The one who forgives will in fact gradually be able to overcome lingering feelings of bitterness or resentment, and replace them

with others. The first and essential step is not to allow oneself to be ruled by such emotions.

The Sacrament of Reconciliation [pp.175–177]
Two important points are made on p.175:

- the distinction between 'mortal' and 'venial' sin;
- the distinction between what is *required* of Catholics in respect of 'Confession' and what they are *encouraged* to do.

Briefly, Catholics are ordinarily required to seek forgiveness for *grave sins* through Confession. They are encouraged to go to confession regularly, even if they have committed no grave sins—because *all* sins are forgiven through the Sacrament, and because it is a great help to progress in the Christian life, and a safeguard against gradually falling away from God.

It has always been the case that Catholics *need* only 'go to confession' before receiving Holy Communion, if they have been guilty of grave sin. Nevertheless, one should, of course, approach Holy Communion in a spirit of penitence for all one's sins. The principal features of the rite which need to be stressed are:

- CONTRITION (sorrow for sin), without which all else is pointless;
- CONFESSION of sins to the priest;
- ABSOLUTION (communication of forgiveness) by the priest;
- PENANCE given by the priest.

The Seal of Confession
The *absolute* confidentiality of confession should be stressed. Even the most confidential secrets may be disclosed in certain circumstances for very grave and pressing reasons. The great exception is Sacramental Confession. Under no circumstances, for any reason whatsoever, may a priest ever betray what a penitent has revealed in Confession.

Difficult but Useful [p.177]
The points made here may be useful as a basis for discussion.

4. Use and Abuse of Gifts [pp.178–185]

This subsection deals, in an outline fashion, successively with: use of one's own gifts, use of and attitudes to material possessions, treatment of the created world, abuse of drugs or alcohol.

The text on p.178 is a prescribed text.

Questions [p.178]

1. 100%

2. 100%

3. Nil

4. Neither. Both did as well as each other.

5. Because he had no profit to show; he might as well not have received anything for all the use he had made of it.

Parable of the Rich Fool [p.181]
This, together with the following passage (Lk. 12:22–31) is a prescribed text.

Questions

1. In this case, greed for possessions

2. His only concern is with his riches and the selfish use he can make of them. He finds his security in them.

3. Because riches can give no lasting security. They have no lasting value for anyone, and in this case he is not given even a short time to enjoy them.

4. They should not regard them as the main thing in life. They should not have a selfish attitude towards them. They should not put their trust in them.

Questions [p.182]

1. The Kingdom of God.

2. A variety of possible answers.

Stewards of the World [pp.183–4]
Christianity in general, and Catholic belief in particular, does not see the human race as just another species, merely one of the many

creatures which inhabit the earth. Humanity stands apart as the summit of material creation, specially chosen and endowed by God, and called to union with him. (This theme will be further pursued in Unit 5.) The World is made for Man, and he can use it for his benefit, but that does not mean that he can use it irresponsibly or without respect for it as God's handiwork.

Things to Do   [p.184]
Though there will not be time to go into great detail, it is helpful if pupils have some basic ideas about the sources of pollution. It is preferable to concentrate on areas on which opinion is most generally agreed and most securely based, rather than on the more speculative analyses and prognostications.

Abuse of Drugs and Alcohol
Under this rubric can, of course, be included such things as glue/solvent-sniffing. The treatment is very general. Its main aim is to promote awareness of the moral case against such addiction. The key idea, though not the only one, is enslavement. Addiction of this nature, in addition to its serious physical effects, involves a major loss of freedom and control in the conduct of one's life and the regulation of one's actions. It brings with it a corruption of the personality and of one's personal integrity. There are numerous official publications on this area which will provide necessary data. The chief concern, however, should be to promote awareness of the principles involved, rather than the acquisition of a wide range of empirical data for its own sake.

Questions   [p.185]
1.   Normally the first two and the last reasons apply.

2.   Yes, insofar as it makes it harder to live as one should, and poses great danger of causing us to harm or otherwise fail in our duty to our neighbour.

3.   Yes, because it makes us less capable of using our talents and abilities in the way we should, and may cause us to let them go to waste completely.

4.   It exposes one to grave danger of seriously damaging one's own personal freedom, of becoming enslaved, and ready to do anything to feed one's addiction. It exposes one to the

danger of seriously harming one's health, and bringing about premature death, of ruining one's life and squandering one's talents, of bringing grief to one's relatives and friends, and possibly having harmful effects on other members of one's family.

Catechism of the Catholic Church

The following are some of the articles from the Catchism which may be found useful in regard to topics dealt with in the Student Text or referred to in this Teacher's Guide.

God as Love and the Source of Love (218–221. 257, 260, 733); Love as Gift and Fundamental Law (1822–1829, 1965–1974, 2054–55, 2093–4); Prayer in general (2558–2751); Lord's Prayer (2759–2865); Sources of Morality (1750–1756); Conscience (1776–1797); Sin (1846–1876); Dishonesty in Word (2464–2522); Dishonesty in Deed (2401–2414); Social Justice & Attitudes to Material Possessions (1928–1948, 2437–2449, 2534–2557); Mercy and Forgiveness (1829, 2838–2845); Sacrament of Reconcilliation (1422–1470); Stewardship of Creation (2415–2418); Abuse of Drugs, etc. (2288–2291).

UNIT 4

THE CHURCH

Section A : The Nature of the Church

This Section deals successively with the topics detailed in the syllabus content, and includes treatment of the texts prescribed in connection with these, as appropriate. In the outline below, indication is given of the subsections in which *texts prescribed in the syllabus* occur.

Outline of Section A

1. *The Beginnings*
    The Apostles, Pentecost and after
    St Paul
    SUMMARY
    Texts: *Mk 3:13–19; Acts 2:37–41, 9:1–22*

2. *The People of God*
    Holy, Priestly and Prophetic
    SUMMARY
    Texts: *1 Pet 2:9–10*

3. *The Body of Christ*
    One Body of many parts
    With Christ as Head
    SUMMARY
    Texts: *Eph 4:4–7,11–13,(14–16); 1 Cor 12:12–31*

4. *The Sacrament of Christ*
    The idea of Sacrament: Sign and Instrument
    The Church represents Christ
    Ways in which the Church is sacramental
    Keeping the sign clear
    SUMMARY

5. *Communion of Saints*
    Communion of the faithful on earth
    The Saints and the faithful departed

6. *The Blessed Virgin Mary*
    Her place in the Church and her relationship to its members
    Texts: *Jn 19:25–27*

7.   *One, Holy, Catholic & Apostolic*
     Texts: Article of the Creed

This Unit presumes understanding of the main themes covered in
Unit 1. The Catholic understanding of the Church—as the means
through which Jesus continues to proclaim his message and
communicate his salvation—clearly requires this. It may be
advisable, before commencing the topics specified in the syllabus,
first of all to have a preliminary session in which pupils may be
encouraged to surface their existing understanding of the Church's
nature and function, and to discuss the extent of any existing
connection and involvement with it. For example:

- a brain-storming session in which pupils suggest words,
  expressions which reflect something which they think is
  connected with what the Church is, or which comes to mind
  when the word 'church' is mentioned.

- These could be recorded on a blackboard or flip chart, and then
  subsequently discussed with the class. They could be grouped
  according to whether they referred to the Church's nature (what
  it is), its purpose (what it is for), and attitudes/reactions towards
  it or opinions concerning it. In some cases categories may
  overlap.

1. The Beginnings   [pp.189–193]

Mark 3:13–19 (given on p.189), Acts 2:37–41,42 (p.190) are
prescribed texts. The account of the Descent of the Holy Spirit, in
Acts 2:1–4, (in the margin of p.190) is not prescribed. It is
included here simply for reference.

Questions (top)   [p.190]

1.   Repent and be baptized.

2.   Forgiveness of sins, gift of the Holy Spirit.

3.   Jesus came to bring forgiveness and to make people children
     of God through the gift of the Spirit. The answer is not
     directly contained in the text. It requires knowledge of Unit 1
     (pp.38–40, 43–45).

Activity
The point of both these suggested activities is to promote understanding of the transformation brought about by the events of Pentecost.

The Early Church after Pentecost
The key point to note here is that from the beginning the Church is characterized by:

- dependence on the guidance and teaching of the Apostles, appointed by Jesus,

- the celebration of the Eucharist, instituted by Jesus.

Questions (bottom)

1. *Koinonia* implies a general family/community spirit of sharing and mutual involvement, which would be manifested in many aspects of corporate or communal activity. Underlying all, however, was the basic 'common possession', a common faith in and commitment to the Lord Jesus, a common life in the Spirit. The unity principally involved therefore is the unity of faith and love.

2. Because they were appointed by Jesus, and taught with his authority.

3. At the Last Supper by Jesus himself, on the night before he was crucified.

The Twelve Apostles and St Paul [p.191]
One point in the material on St Paul is that he is not a self-appointed Apostle. Although not one of the 'Twelve' appointed by Jesus during his earthly life, he is regarded as someone with the same kind of apostolic authority, because it is given him by the risen Christ. Acts 9:1–22 (pp.191–192) is a prescribed text.

Questions [p.193]

1. In order to arrest Christians.

2. Jesus identifies himself with his Church. To persecute them is to persecute him.

3. He prayed. He did not eat or drink.

4.   The events had had a profound spiritual effect on Paul.
     Prayer and fasting are, among other things, signs of
     repentance.

5.   He was baptized.

6.   'He is the Son of God.'

7.   Because he had been such a fierce persecutor of Christians
     until only a short time before.

Overview and Background Notes to Subsections 2–4

These subsections deal successively with these images of the
Church: People of God, Body of Christ, and Sacrament of Christ.
They are interconnected.

A.   The image of People of God, points to the continuity of the
     Church with the Old Testament chosen people of God, Israel.
     It represents the Church as the People of the New Covenant
     in Christ, which fulfils and perfects the Old. Unlike the old
     Israel, membership of this new people is open to men and
     women of all nations. The criterion now is not ancestry, but
     faith in Christ. It is an image which stresses community.
     Christians are not just a collection of isolated individuals, but
     a community, with a common life and destiny, in which all
     are involved.

     It is a community which, of its nature, is holy, priestly and
     prophetic. These are qualities which pertain to the Church as
     such, and therefore all members participate in them. All are
     called to reflect the Church's holiness in the holiness of their
     lives, to participate in its 'priestly' and 'prophetic' functions.
     This image therefore is concerned with what is true of all
     members of the Church.

B.   The image of the Body of Christ is also concerned with unity
     and oneness, but here the emphasis is on organic unity,
     within which there is diversity of gifts and functions. It deals
     not only with what all have in common, but also the
     differences which exist between various members, and with

how, nevertheless, these differences not only do not destroy unity, but build it up.

The analogy of the co-operative inter-dependence of the various parts of the body is well adapted to convey the idea of the Church as an organically structured unity, of which all are equally members, though performing different roles. Because it involves the idea of Christ as the Head of this Body, it also expresses more clearly than the image of the People of God the intimacy of the relationship between Christ and the Church, and the essential distinction between the people of the New Covenant and the Old.

C.   The two images need to be taken together in order to gain a balanced picture. Members of the Church do have different gifts, roles, functions, as the image of the 'Body of Christ' emphasizes, but nevertheless each in his or her own way is called to take part not only in some small specialised area of the Church's activity, but in the whole of its life and mission. This is what is implicit in the image of the Church as People of God. For example, bishops have particular functions as teachers of the faith that are not common to all, but nevertheless all are called to participate in some way in the Church's mission of witnessing to and proclaiming the truth. Priests have particular priestly functions which they alone can perform, but nevertheless all are called to participate in their own way in the general 'priestly' character of the Church, through prayer, worship and the offering of their own lives and actions to God. The image of the 'Body of Christ' emphasizes interdependence of differing functions and gifts in one community.

The image of the 'People of God' emphasizes that, nevertheless, all have a role to play in all areas of Church life. The two images are complementary rather than antagonistic.

D.   The idea of the Church as the 'Sacrament' of Christ is not the same as the image of the 'Body of Christ', but the latter image does at least provide a jumping-off point, as will be seen in the Student Text. The idea of the Church as

'Sacrament' is a key one. In many ways it sums up admirably fundamental Catholic teaching on the Church, its relationship to Christ, its mission and function. The basic ideas are given on p.200 and need not be repeated here.

2. The People of God [pp.194–196]

1 Peter 2:9–10 is a prescribed text. This image portrays the Church as the successor of Israel, the Old Testament People of God.

Questions [p.195]

1. The 'darkness' is the darkness of alienation from God, of sin, of error, ignorance, fear etc. The 'light' is the light of truth, faith, love, mercy etc. Christians are brought out of the darkness of sin and error into the light of faith in Christ and love of God.

2. (a) They have received God's forgiveness.
   (b) Through faith, repentance and baptism.
   (c) Because they are no longer separated from him, because he has redeemed them.

Priesthood
More is said on this matter in Section B (p.239).

3. The Body of Christ [pp.197–199]

The two extracts from Ephesians (4:4–6,7 and 4:13) are both prescribed texts. In these extracts there is great emphasis on Unity or Oneness.

Questions [p.197]

1. Eternal life with Christ.

2. Jesus Christ.

3. They believe the same things; they have a common set of beliefs.

One Body [p.198]
The passage from 1 Corinthians (12:12–31) is a prescribed text. It is not essential for pupils to explore all the intricacies of Paul's

analogy. All that is necessary is an understanding of the main thrust of his argument.

Questions

1. Baptism.

2. Not all the parts of the body have the same function, but they still all belong to the body. They all have a part to play and depend upon each other. The health of the body depends on the harmonious working of all the different parts which go to make up the one body. It is the same with the Church. Members have different gifts and roles, but they are all important, and all have an important part to play for the good of the whole.

Christ the Head [p.199]

The passage from Ephesians (which is part of a prescribed text) illustrates the main points made here. It reads as follows:

> '... so that we may no longer be children, tossed to and fro and carried about by every wind of doctrine, by the cunning of men, by their craftiness in deceitful wiles. Rather, speaking the truth in love, we are to grow up in every way into him who is the Head, into Christ, from whom the whole body, joined and knit together by every joint with which it is supplied, when each part is working properly, makes bodily growth and upbuilds itself in love.' (Eph. 4:14–16)

4. *The Sacrament of Christ* [pp.200–202]

The idea of the Church as the Sacrament (i.e. Sign and Instrument) of Christ and his salvation is a key one, and it is important that it is thoroughly understood by pupils. Salvation was won by Christ, and is proclaimed and communicated by him through the Church in every generation. The important basic definition of Sacrament is as a sign which both reveals something and puts it into effect. Through the Church, Christ reveals (makes known) himself and his salvation, and communicates that salvation to the people of the world across the ages.

5. *The Communion of Saints* [p.203]

Questions

1. This calls for a personal response.

2. This also calls for a personal response.

3. 2nd November, All Souls' Day: Commemoration of All the Faithful Departed.

4. This might be found encouraging and inspiring. It might help people to see how they should live, and what they should consider important.

6. *The Blessed Virgin Mary* [pp.204–5]

In Catholic teaching, the relationship of Mary to the rest of the Church is based upon her relationship to Christ. Mary, the Mother of Jesus, is considered also to be the mother of all those whom he has made his brothers and sisters, as children of God. It is Mary's unique role in the work of salvation, and her unique relationship to Jesus which gives her a unique place and role in the Communion of Saints.

[p.205]   John 19:25–27 is a prescribed text.

Questions

1. (a) Because the one to whom she gave birth was not only a human child, but also truly God.
    (b) Because every Christian should pray not just for himself/herself, but for all members of the Church, and indeed for all people. The 'Our Father' (the Lord's Prayer).
    (c) It should be unselfish and concerned for others. It is made by someone not just as an individual, but as a member of the Church, the People of God and the Body of Christ.
    (d) Because that is when they go to meet God.

2. Because the one who gives them power to become children of God was himself born of her. Because she is the mother of Jesus, and they are his brothers and sisters.

7. *One, Holy, Catholic and Apostolic* [pp.206 –207]

These four 'marks' or 'notes' of the Church have in fact been anticipated in the previous material.

Revision [p.207]

The questions draw attention to how each of them has been considered previously in the Student Text.

1. See especially pp.197–199.

2. See especially pp.194–195.

3. The word 'saint' means 'holy'. Christians are considered to be 'holy' in the sense that they have been chosen and consecrated by God and have received the gift of the Holy Spirit. They are called to be holy in their lives.

4. The fact that he sought to preach the Gospel to all nations.

5. See especially pp.189–193.

Catechism of the Catholic Church

The following are some of the articles from the Catechism which may be found useful in regard to topics dealt with in this Section.

People of God (781–785); Body of Christ (787–795); Church as Sacrament (771–776); Communion of Saints (946–959); The Blessed Virgin Mary and the Church (963–972); One, Holy Catholic and Apostolic (811–865)

Section B

Mission and Life of the Church

This Section deals successively with the topics detailed in the syllabus content, and includes treatment of the texts prescribed in connection with these, as appropriate. As in Section A, in the outline given below, indication is only given of where texts *prescribed in the syllabus* occur.

Outline of Section B

1. *The Magnificat*
   Texts: *Lk 1:39–55*

2. *Programmes for Action*
   Texts: *Mt 28:16–20; Acts 1:5,8*

3. The Sacraments

4. *Sacraments of Initiation — Baptism*
   Symbolism
   Baptism of children
   Adoption, Dying and Rising with Christ
   Faith and Repentance
   Texts: *Jn 3:5; Rom 6:3–4*

5. *Sacraments of Initiation — Confirmation*
   Completion of Baptism
   The Minister
   The Rite

6. *The Holy Eucharist — The Mass as Sacrifice*
   The Mass
   Roles of priest and people
   The account of St Paul
   Texts: *1 Cor 11:23–26*

7. *The Celebration of Mass*
   Liturgy of the Word
   Liturgy of The Eucharist

8. *The Holy Eucharist — A Sacred Meal — Holy Communion*
    The Eucharist as a meal — the presence of Christ
    The Bread of Life — Holy Communion
    SUMMARY
    Texts: *1 Cor 10:16, 17; 11:27, 29; Jn 6:48–58*

9. *Vocation and Ministry*
    Ordained ministers: bishop, priest, deacon
    Parish lay ministries
    National Catholic Associations
    Religious Orders
    Priesthood in general
    Texts: *Roman Missal: Preface of the Priesthood (Chrism Mass)*

10. *Teaching Authority*
    Scripture and Tradition — Apostolic Authority
    The place of Peter — the Pope
    Infallibility
    Texts: *Mt 10:40, 16:13–19, 18:18; Jn 21:15–19*

11. *Ecumenism*
    The meaning and purposes of Ecumenism
    The Catholic Church and other churches

1. The Magnificat [pp.208–209]

In Section A there was treatment of the Catholic view of Mary as a kind of spiritual mother. Here we deal with the complementary Catholic view of her role as model and exemplar of what the Church is and is called to be, as a model of Christian faith and of the attitudes which the Church as a whole, and every individual Christian, should have. The *Magnificat* is taken as the starting point. The two extracts on these pages from the Gospel of Luke, (altogether 1:39–55), are both prescribed texts.

Questions (first set) [p.209]

1. Practically the whole hymn is a song of rejoicing, e.g. 'My spirit rejoices in God my Saviour.' (Incidentally, the name 'Jesus' means 'Saviour') Also, 'For behold henceforth all

generations will call me blessed', and 'For he who is mighty has done great things for me.' Anything from: 'And his mercy is on those who fear him...' to the end.

2. Humble: 'He has regarded the low estate of his handmaid'. Grateful: 'He who is mighty has done great things for me'.

3. God.

4. The humble and the poor.

5. They should have a spirit of humility and not be attached to worldly riches. They should have concern for the poor and lowly.

Questions (second set)

1. The importance of Mary's role as mother of Jesus; the importance of her faith.

2. Mary's faith and God's choice of her were both gifts that came from God. Both were blessings that came from him. Mary could not have become Mother of the Lord without God's choice of her. But equally she would not have become Mother of the Lord without freely accepting in faith God's choice of her. The blessing of her faith was a necessary condition for the blessing of becoming Mother of God. The two are interconnected.

2. Programmes for Action   (pp.210–211)

All of the Scriptural extracts on p.210 (Mt 28:16–20 and Acts 1:5,8) are prescribed texts.

Questions   [p.210]

1. The Apostles: there were only eleven because Judas Iscariot, who betrayed Jesus, had committed suicide.

2. Something on the lines of 'Make people of all nations Christians, i.e. followers of Jesus.

3. 'Catholic' means 'universal' This command makes it clear that the Church has to proclaim the Gospel to everyone, and

be open to people of every race and nationality. The message is universal. It is meant for everyone.

4. Because 'all authority in heaven and earth has been given' to him. Because he is the Lord of all and Saviour of all, his salvation is for all nations.

5. 'I am with you always, to the close of the age.'

6. It shows that the Church is the special instrument through which Christ makes himself known and through which he communicates his salvation.

Questions [p.211]

1. Preaching and teaching, being examples of faith, readiness to suffer persecution or martyrdom.

2. 'Go therefore and make disciples of all nations.' 'You shall be my witnesses... to the ends of the earth.'

3. The Sacraments [p.212]

The statement concerning the nature of the Sacraments in the left-hand column should be carefully noted. In particular, it should be explained that, in Catholic teaching, Sacraments are not merely celebrations of what Jesus has done, but the actual means through which Jesus himself communicates the fruits of salvation. Sacraments are performed through the ministry of the Church, but it is Jesus Christ himself, by the power of the Holy Spirit, who makes them effective. For the purposes of examination on this Unit, pupils need have only an outline knowledge of the nature and purpose of the four Sacraments described in the right hand column. What is given there would be enough.

4. Sacraments of Initiation — Baptism [pp.213–219]

The initial quotation from John is a prescribed text. Emphasis should be given to the distinction between the baptism of John and Christian baptism. The first was primarily an expression of repentance. The second, because it is a Sacrament, is primarily a sign of what God is doing for the one being baptized. It is the means through which God acts.

The Symbolism of Baptism

The syllabus requires only attention to the essential symbolic features: the pouring on or immersion in water, and the accompanying words. Other secondary features (including anointing with Chrism, white garment and lighted candle) need not be dealt with for examination purposes. In baptism, as in all Sacraments, the words and symbolic actions essential to the celebration of the Sacrament are signs of what Jesus is doing for the people being baptized. Careful attention should be given to the dual symbolism of water. The Scriptural quotations in the margins are not prescribed texts. They are included merely as examples of how the imagery of water is used in both Old and New Testaments. It is an imagery which deals with water as both a symbol of cleansing and a symbol of life.

Divergent views

The syllabus requires some reference to main features of divergent views held by other Christians on this matter. It is for this reason that specific attention is given to certain aspects of the question of infant baptism, and to the question of baptism by immersion versus infusion (pouring). It may be added that some protestant Christians would consider baptism to be primarily or simply a symbolic ceremony expressive of the faith and commitment of the one being baptized. This derives from a different view of the nature and function of sacraments.

Why Baptize Children?   [p.214]

This brief treatment provides an exposition of Catholic teaching on the baptism of infants, and in particular of how it can be considered as a 'washing away' of sin. Briefly, all sin involves separation from God. Personal sins involve personal wrongdoing and personal guilt. This is not the case with what is called the state of 'Original Sin', but it is still a kind of separation from God which comes from the sinful history of the human race. It is in that restricted sense that it is called 'sin', and implies no personal guilt on the part of the child. In giving a share in God's life as his children, baptism simultaneously takes away this separation. The following material on 'Adoption' (p.215) further explicates the point, and may be found to be the most effective way of conveying the essential idea.

The Catholic practice of infant baptism (by no means confined to Catholics) emphasizes that the Sacrament is primarily a work of God through Jesus Christ. It represents God's choice and God's undeserved gift. Further material on arguments for and against infant baptism are given on p.218. It should be emphasized that, though in infant baptism the Sacrament is often celebrated not long after birth, it is not to be considered a celebration of the child's natural birth, nor simply as a ceremony of welcome into the church community. In Catholic teaching, baptism at any age or stage of life is a spiritual 'rebirth' as a child of God, and the actual means by which someone, through being united with Jesus, is made a member of his Body, the Church. It is not therefore simply a 'rite of passage' marking a particular phase of life.

The Words used in Baptism   [p.216]
In addition to the central symbolic features mentioned earlier, the syllabus requires attention to the words used in the actual 'formula' of baptism. The text seeks to elucidate why it is appropriate to mention all three Person of the Blessed Trinity. Pupils should know the baptismal formula.

Questions

1.   Individual answers. It is the reasons which are important.

2.   Among the reasons, some of the following might be mentioned:
     – Since baptism is not simply a private matter, but makes someone a member of the Church, it is appropriate for the whole community (or a great many of them) to be present.
     – It encourages community feeling, and a sense of responsibility towards children in the Church.
     – It helps to remind people of the importance and meaning of their own baptism.

4.   The essential point, however expressed, is that in baptism we are united with Jesus as his brothers and sisters by the work of the Spirit, and so can call his Father 'Our Father'.

United with Jesus in his Death and Resurrection
The quotation from Romans (6:3–4) is a prescribed text.

Question [p.217]
This aims to draw out something about the implications of living 'a new life'. One way of doing this might be to take examples from history of conversions which radically changed a person's life, e.g. in Scripture, Zacchaeus or St Paul. Extra-biblical examples could include those who changed radically on actually becoming a Christian and being baptized (e.g. St Augustine), or who changed radically, when they began to try really to live out the baptism they had received earlier (e.g. St Francis, St Katherine of Genoa, St Ignatius Loyola, Charles de Foucauld). Alternatively, or in addition, one could perhaps find someone baptized as an adult who could explain what difference it made to his/her life.

Total Immersion
Some pupils may be surprised to learn that this method of baptism is even today possible in the Catholic Church. In fact, it is becoming more common, though it is still not nearly the most common method. Some new churches are deliberately built with a baptismal pool for this purpose. In some very ancient churches, including the basilica of St Paul Outside the Walls in Rome, there still survive ancient baptisteries which have provision for what was once obviously a great pool of water into which those who were to be baptized descended. It may be possible to obtain photographs or slides showing these. However, baptism by pouring was also used from very early times. In some places, circumstances might make it the only practicable option. The practice of baptizing by pouring water on the head is mentioned in a very early Christian written work called the Didache. It probably virtually superseded the practice of immersion for mainly practical reasons. The Catholic Church teaches that both methods are equally valid, and both are permissible.

Discuss
The chief argument in favour is that it expresses more fully the meaning of baptism in regard to 'dying with Christ' and 'rising to new life', and is a more dramatic expression of the 'cleansing' function of baptism. The chief arguments against are mainly

practical. Some of them would have had particular force in some former ages, especially in Northern European countries in Winter!

Faith and Repentance
Another element of the baptismal ritual specifically mentioned in the syllabus is 'renunciation of sin and profession of faith'. Pupils therefore need to know about these and their significance. An important basic point is that, in Catholic teaching, baptism embodies a gift from God, but it is a gift that can be refused. This can come about through refusal to believe or refusal to turn away from sin. Baptism involves forgiveness of sins, and so for those capable of personal sin, a readiness to renounce sin is required. One cannot deliberately remain on the side of sin if one wants to be on the side of God. For examination purposes, pupils only need to know about these consideration and about preparation for baptism, in general terms. The details about the catechumenate given in the marginal note are included only as additional information.

Infant Baptism [p.218]
This material is included in order to deal with one of the differences in practice etc. between various groups of Christians mentioned in the syllabus. Those other Christians who argue against infant baptism usually base their arguments on one or both of the following considerations:

(a) Baptism presumes and requires personal faith, of which infants are incapable.

(b) It is the child's right to choose for himself/herself, and this can only be done at a later stage.

In regard to (a), Catholic teaching would say that what is needed is openness to God's gifts, including faith. While a child cannot, in a personal responsible way, positively *accept* such gifts, it can nevertheless *receive* them, and indeed is not capable of refusing. God's gifts are meant for all humanity, including children. In time, the child will have, on his/her own account, to make a personal act of faith, but will then do so as one already included in God's family, already under the influence of his grace. Baptism of infants therefore is a great gift and blessing for them, and something which Christian parents should be anxious to ensure for their children, and which the Church should be anxious to provide.

With regard to (b), Catholic teaching would say that there is no infringement of a child's rights, any more than there is in regard to the many other responsible decisions which parents have to make for the benefit of their children. Like anyone else, a baptized child, as he/she grows up, will become increasingly responsible for deciding whether or not to accept or to continue to accept Christian beliefs and values. The fact of baptism does not take that away. In the long run, it will still be his/her decision. A related argument concerns the question of religious education or catechesis. Some would argue that it is better not to give children a Christian religious education, so that they can choose freely what to believe, when they become older. A contrary argument is that Christian parents who really believe will want to give their children the best, and for them this will be Christianity. In the end, the children will have to make their own decision, but in the meantime the parents have a duty to bring them up in the best way they know. After all, good parents will teach their children not to steal, lie, injure others etc. Should they keep quiet about such things, and simply let their children decide whether to become thieves, liars and murderers when they grow up? In the long run, some may end up like that anyway, but is it an infringement of their freedom to influence them in other ways while they are growing up? If not, is not the same true about a religious upbringing?

The mere fact of Christian parents not trying to give their children a religious upbringing may well be a kind of education in another direction. It conveys the idea that matters of faith are not really very important. A person who really values honesty would not keep quiet about it to his children or fail to try to influence them to be honest. These kinds of question need to be discussed with pupils. Pupils should also be aware of the responsibilities assumed by parents and godparents who bring a child for baptism.

Additional Note [p.219]
The details of emergency baptism are given merely as additional information.

5. Sacraments of Initiation — Confirmation   [pp.220 – 221]

Pupils need only know the outlines of the rite: prayer said by a bishop over candidates (asking for the gifts of the Holy Spirit), anointing on the forehead with chrism, with the accompanying words. Fundamentally, they need to understand that Confirmation is considered a kind of additional 'sealing' or strengthening of the consecration of baptism, which binds those being confirmed more firmly to the faith, life and mission of the Church. The gifts of the Holy Spirit are permanent gifts, to help them live as active, faithful members of Christ's Body, the Church.

Additional Activities
The following might be suggested:

1. Write out a list of the gifts of the Holy Spirit. Against each say how it might help a Christian to be true to his/her baptism.

2. Make a poster/display illustrating the meaning of the use of chrism in Confirmation.

The Holy Eucharist

Subsections 6, 7 and 8 together deal with the Eucharist. 6 deals with the basic meaning and significance of Mass, concentrating mainly on the Mass as Sacrifice. This is basic to the Catholic understanding. 7 deals with liturgical details of the celebration of Mass. 8 deals with the Mass considered as a Sacred Meal, and especially with the meaning and significance of Holy Communion. All thee are interconnected and very important.

6. The Holy Eucharist — The Mass as Sacrifice   [pp.223–225]

As a preliminary, it may be useful to revise quickly the events of the Last Supper (Unit 2, especially p.62). The *key points* of this subsection in regard to Catholic teaching are:

• On the Cross Jesus offered himself totally to his Father to atone for our sins.

- The Mass is the means he gave his Church of continually participating in that offering.

That is why the Mass is considered to be the greatest possible act of worship and thanksgiving. The idea, contained in the last paragraph of this subsection in the Student Text, that it is also the means of promoting an imitation of Jesus's attitude of self-giving for others, should also be stressed.

The Roles of Priest and People [p.224]

This item, which is specifically mentioned in the syllabus, is not in the nature of an aside, but is integral to the Catholic understanding of the Mass as participation in the offering of Christ's sacrifice. The presiding bishop or priest is considered to be the visible representation of Jesus Christ. It is through him that the invisible presence of Christ, the true High Priest, is visibly expressed, and through him that Christ, by the power of the Holy Spirit, makes the bread and wine his Body and Blood, and makes the offering of his sacrifice in a visible manner. The bishop or priest is here acting not in his own name, but in the name of Christ, and not in his own person, but 'in the person of Christ'. He is therefore the *visible sign and instrument* through whom Christ makes his presence known and through whom he makes the eternal offering of his sacrifice present and available for the Church's participation.

He is therefore a *sacramental* figure. It is for this reason that it is the bishop or the priest alone, as representing Christ to the members of his Body, the Church, who says the words of the Eucharistic Prayer. All this emphasises that the Eucharist is, in the first place, the action of Christ. It is *his* Eucharist, in which the Church participates.

The Account of St Paul [p.224]

The quotation from 1 Corinthians (11:23–26) is a prescribed text. It forms part of a reproof to the Corinthians for their lack of respect towards the Eucharistic celebration. Paul here is trying to explain what is so special about it. The following may be noted: 'I received from the Lord'. This is in fact part of the traditional teaching Paul has received. Paul seems here to equate receiving the authentic apostolic tradition with receiving something 'from the

Lord.' The teaching of the Lord is present in the tradition of the Church.

Questions [p.225]

1. The last verse: 'For as often as you eat... you proclaim the Lord's death....'

2. 'On the night he was betrayed' The Eucharist was instituted just before Jesus's Crucifixion.

3. In celebrating the Eucharist, they are joining in the celebration of Jesus's sacrificial death. (This is because the 'bread' is the body of Jesus, given for them, and the cup is the 'new covenant' in his blood.)

4. The cup of blessing (see Unit 2, p.62).

5. The 'New Covenant' is the new relationship between God and human beings, established by Jesus. This new relationship is brought about, and won for human beings, by Jesus's self-offering on behalf of mankind (i.e. his Crucifixion). It is brought about therefore by the shedding of his blood (again see Unit 2, p.62).

7. *The Celebration of Mass* [pp.226–230]

It should be noted that the syllabus only requires 'an outline knowledge of the broad structure of the Mass and the most important elements of the Eucharistic Prayer'. For examination purposes therefore it is not necessary for pupils to know every detail in this subsection. They should know:

*   the general nature and purpose of the Penitential Rite (but not necessarily details of its possible variations);
*   the general nature, content and function of the Liturgy of the Word (but not necessarily all the permutations or minor details);
*   the general outline of the Liturgy of the Eucharist: Preparation of the Gifts (offertory), Eucharistic Prayer, Communion.

In regard to the Eucharistic Prayer itself, they should have an outline knowledge of the general nature and function of the:

*   variable preface leading into 'Holy, Holy, Holy...';

- Epiclesis;
- Consecration (Words of Institution);
- Memorial/Offertory;
- final Doxology, followed by Great Amen.

They should be aware that the Prayer does include prayers for the living and the dead. They should know the special significance of the Great Amen, as the principal *external* way in which the members of the congregation associate themselves with the offering and the intercessions. They should also know some other ways in which the congregation externally participates in the celebration at any stage.

An outline of the Mass is also given at the beginning of Unit 2 (p.50). It may be found useful for giving a general picture, but knowledge of all the details given in it will not be necessary for examination purposes.

Copies of the Missal will be found useful. Alternatively (and cheaply), if any local parishes use 'missalettes' or have used them in the past, it may be possible to obtain copies from them at little or no cost. Such publications may also be purchased cheaply from certain firms, including: 'Jerusalem Mass Sheet' (Catholic Printing Co. of Farnworth). These kinds of publication can exemplify for pupils the shape and structure of the celebration. The best way, however, is attendance at the celebration of Mass, particularly the main Sunday Mass at a parish church.

Among videos which may be found useful are:

- *Mass of the Roman Rite*, a recording of an actual normative celebration: Veritas Video;
- *Understanding the Liturgy of the Mass*, Liguori (an American production, available from both Veritas and Redemptorist Publications).

Things to Do   [p . 230]

4.   Because the Mass is the celebration of Jesus's offering of himself to God the Father for our sake.

8. *The Holy Eucharist — A Sacred Meal — Holy Communion*
[pp.231–234]

Subsection 6 dealt with the Eucharist as Sacrifice. This subsection deals with the complementary idea of the Eucharist as a Sacred Meal. In the left-hand column of p.231 a relatively straightforward exposition of Catholic (and Eastern Orthodox) doctrine is given, avoiding technical language. The technical term for the Eucharistic transformation ('transubstantiation') need not be known by pupils for examination purposes.

One example of the Church's belief from earliest times in the 'real presence' of Jesus Christ in the Eucharist is contained in the writings of St Justin Martyr. St Justin, writing in about A.D. 150, says, 'We do not receive these things as common bread and common drink; but just as our Saviour Jesus Christ, being incarnate through the word of God, took flesh and blood for our salvation, so too we have been taught that the food over which thanksgiving have been made (literally 'which has been eucharistized')... is both the flesh and blood of that incarnate Jesus' (Justin, *Apologia 66, 2*). It is worth adding (though candidates will not be asked questions specifically on this) that the phrase 'body and blood' taken together means Jesus Christ in his entirety. Moreover, it is Catholic belief that, though the appearances of bread symbolize 'the body' and the appearances of wine symbolize 'the blood' which was shed, in reality the risen Jesus who is received in Holy Communion cannot be divided up in this way. In actual fact Jesus Christ in his entirety is present under the appearances of either bread or wine alone.

The right hand-column of p.231 contains other views on the Eucharist . There are many varieties of such rival views, but these are fairly typical and representative of those who see *merely* a symbolic meaning in the words of Jesus. Some acquaintance with views which differ from Catholic belief is required by the syllabus.

The Bread of Life [p.232]
The quotation from John 6 on this page is a prescribed text. The first paragraph in the material in the Student Text refers to the scandalisation of many of Jesus's hearers. These in fact included some of Jesus's disciples. St John's Gospel says that, after this

episode, many of Jesus's disciples left him. Jesus asked the Apostles if they would go away also, and Peter replied, 'Lord, to whom shall we go? You have the words of eternal life.' (Jn 6:66–69)

Questions

1. 'I am the Bread of Life.'; 'I am the living Bread which came down from heaven.'; 'The bread that I will give ... is my flesh.'

2. It gives eternal life. 'Your fathers ate the manna in the desert and they died. This is the bread that comes down from heaven, which a man may eat and not die.'; 'If anyone eats of this bread, he will live for ever.' etc.

3. No. He repeats it emphatically. 'Truly, truly, I say to you, unless you eat the flesh of the Son of Man and drink his blood, you have no life in you.'

4. Not really. He explains what the effects of 'eating his flesh and drinking his blood' will be, but he does not otherwise explain his words.

5. This is a matter for discussion with pupils. For Christians who believe in the real presence of Jesus in the Eucharist the message is fairly obvious. How might other Christians interpret it ?

Holy Communion [p.233]

The first paragraph adverts to an important point. In Catholic belief, after the consecration, only the *appearances* (Latin, '*species*') of bread and wine remain. It is therefore strictly inaccurate to speak, for example of 'bread and wine' symbolizing the Body and Blood of Christ. In print, one may convey what is meant by making the initial letter of 'Bread' and 'Wine' capital, or by putting the words within inverted commas, but this is not something so easily conveyed in speech. When speaking of Catholic belief therefore, teachers would do best to speak of the 'appearances' of bread and the 'appearances' of wine symbolizing the Body and Blood of Christ. Similarly, it is better and more accurate to speak of Christ's presence 'under the appearances of bread and wine', rather than 'in the bread' or 'in the wine'.

The quotation from 1 Corinthians (10:17) is a prescribed text. The point made in relation to this quotation is an important one. 'Communion' refers not just to individual union with Jesus, and through him with the Blessed Trinity, but with all other members of the 'Body of Christ', the Church. The Eucharist is the Sacrament of Unity, i.e. the sign which reveals and deepens the unity of Christ with his Church, and of the members of the Church with each other, through him.

Additional Activity
Make a poster with the title, 'THE BREAD OF LIFE', which expresses the main things Catholics believe about the meaning of Holy Communion.

Receiving Communion [p.234]
(Pupils who are not familiar with the interior of a Catholic Church should visit one, to observe some of the features mentioned in the first paragraph.) The remaining material stresses the importance of Communion for the living of one's life as a Christian. This should be thoroughly discussed with pupils.

Additional Activity
If he/she is sincere, anyone who receives Holy Communion should be wanting to become more like Jesus. What kind of things should they be trying to do? Make a list, and compare it with others in the class.

SUMMARY [p.234]
Teachers may find this helpful in revising main points of Catholic teaching on the Eucharist generally.

9. *Vocation and Ministry* [pp.235–240]

This subsection begins with material on the ordained ministries: bishop, priest, deacon, incorporating only the most basic description of the Sacrament of Holy Orders. Pupils will not need to know any more concerning the liturgy of this Sacrament, for examination purposes. These ordained ministries, since they are conferred through a special Sacrament, have a special position and importance. Bishops and priests especially are vital and necessary elements in the constitution and life of the Church. The bishops are the principal successors of the Apostles and enjoy the fullness of the ministerial priesthood. Priests participate in a subordinate degree in the bishop's ministry, under his authority. In particular, they participate in and exercise the ministerial priesthood, which is a necessary and fundamental element of the Church's being. It is Catholic belief that the role of bishops, and the ministerial priesthood generally, is ordained by God, is an essential feature of the Church, and is a vital part of what makes the Church apostolic.

However, all ordained ministers of the Church have to remember that they are meant to act in a spirit of service. One of the titles of the Pope is 'Servant of the servants of God'. They must seek to help all to use their gifts for the good of all, and must use the authority they have been given in ways that build up the community of faith and in ways which are for the benefit of the People of God, rather than for their own convenience. The fact that bishops and priests have a particularly vital role to perform does not at all mean that the gifts and roles of others are unimportant. The Church cannot flourish without the active involvement of the gifts, abilities and contributions of the various members of the Body of Christ. Where this is not forthcoming, or is discouraged, the Church's life is impoverished and its mission suffers.

Most of the rest of the subsection is concerned with other functions and activities of members of the Church: lay ministries found within parishes, the activities of Catholic Associations and of Religious Orders. There is a wide variety of these, and only an outline treatment is given. For the purposes of the examination paper, pupils need only have a general outline notion of the kind of lay ministries/activities which may usually be found in parishes, some general information about the kind of life and work pursued by 'active' and contemplative Orders and Congregations. No great detail or specificity is required, rather a general representative picture. They should also have some outline information about two or three Catholic Associations.

This portion of the syllabus, however, offers a good opportunity for a deeper inquiry into ministries, a specific Association or a specific Order or Congregation by means of one of the two coursework assignments. Details and addresses of a great variety of Catholic Associations and Religious Orders may be found in the National Catholic Directory, or in the local Diocesan Directory. Many of these, if contacted, will be glad to supply information, literature etc. about their life and activities, and it may be possible for them to arrange for a speaker to come to the school, or for a visit to be made by pupils to some religious house or institution etc. Where Associations have parish branches, a member of, for example, the local SVP might be invited to talk to the pupils. In the case of parish ministries, pupils could also bring in information about which are exercised in their parish, and what they do.

In the event of choosing one of these areas, or indeed any other, to provide a topic for a coursework assignment, teachers should carefully read and digest the Guidelines in the Support Material supplied by the Examining Board.

Videos
One or more of the following may (or may not) be found useful. Priesthood/vocation to the priesthood:

- *Priests* (That's the Spirit);
- *Priesthood* (That's the Spirit);
- *A Slight Change in Plan* (Paulist Productions).

All the above are available from Veritas.

Vocation To The Religious Life:

- *Together for the Gospel* (Liguori) This is an American production. It consists of a series of men and women religious talking about their vocation, and is available from Redemptorist Publications.

Priesthood in General [p.239]
This final part of the subsection seeks first of all to convey the idea that the whole Church, because it is united with Jesus Christ, is 'priestly'. All members of the Church exercise this basic priesthood through prayer, participation in Mass and the Sacraments, and through everything in their lives which gives praise to God. It is because of this priesthood that members of the Church can join in Christ's offering of his Sacrifice in the Eucharist. In addition, and distinct from this in kind, is the

ministerial priesthood (of bishops and priests). The Student Text gives a sufficient explanation of this. The Preface of the Priesthood (p.240) is a prescribed text. It contains reference to Christ as High Priest, and to the common priesthood of the faithful, as well as to the ministerial priesthood. It is a text which usefully summarizes the main elements of the Christian priesthood.

Questions   [p.240]

1.   The new relationship between God and mankind established by Jesus Christ, which will last for ever — including the relationship of children of God.

2.   It means that all are called to participate in Christ's offering of praise and thanksgiving to the Father, especially through prayer, participation in Mass and the Sacraments and in living a life governed by love. (See p.195 of Student Text.)

3.   (a) The celebration of Mass.
     (b) The self-offering of Jesus on the Cross.

4.   The Church; the Eucharist — in particular, Holy Communion.

5.   Proclaiming the Gospel, preaching, teaching.

6.   The bishop's act of placing his hands on the head of the one he is ordaining.

10. Teaching Authority   [pp.241–245]

In the Catholic view, the Church is called to teach all that comes to it from Christ through the Apostles, whether that comes in written form in the inspired Scriptures or otherwise , 'through the spoken word of their preaching, by the example they gave, by the institutions they established' (*Catechism of the Catholic Church, 76*). Consequently, the Catholic Church 'does not derive her certainty about all revealed truths from the holy Scriptures alone' (Vatican II, *Dei Verbum* 9, cf. CCC 82).

The living transmission in its entirety of the Word of God entrusted to the Apostles by Christ and the Holy Spirit is called 'Tradition'. Together, Scripture and Tradition make up a single 'Deposit of faith'.

There are many ways in which the Church can come to a deeper understanding of aspects of the truth committed to it, and many contributions to that understanding can be made by various members of the Church in various capacities, but the Catholic Church teaches that Christ appointed and guaranteed an authoritative teaching body, Peter and the other Apostles, whose authority is transmitted to their successors, the Pope and bishops. It is they who have the authority to interpret the true content and meaning of Christian teaching, determining what is in accordance with the faith and what is contrary to it. In this they have the continuing guidance of the Holy Spirit.

'The task of giving an authentic interpretation of the Word of God, whether in its written form or in the form of Tradition, has been entrusted to the living teaching office of the Church alone. Its authority in this matter is exercised in the name of Jesus Christ. This means that the task of interpretation has been entrusted to the bishops in communion with the successor of Peter, the Bishop of Rome.' (*Dei Verbum* 10, cf. CCC 85).

In the Catholic view therefore, the faithful authoritative transmission of Christian teaching involves three closely connected elements: the Scriptures, general Apostolic Tradition and the authoritative judgments on these made by the Pope and the bishops in communion with him, who form the Teaching Office (*magisterium*) of the Church.

Other Views
This is the Catholic belief, but the syllabus requires some acquaintance with other views on this matter. The following brief notes may help.

The Eastern Orthodox churches, like the Catholic Church, do not confine apostolic tradition to the Scriptures. They pay great regard to the witness to Apostolic Tradition found in the early Church writers known as the 'Fathers' of the Church. They respect the teaching authority of bishops, and accept the decisions of seven great Councils ('Ecumenical Councils') held before the break with Rome (which took place in the eleventh century). Though they are ready to acknowledge that the Pope has a special position in the Church, they do not accept the special doctrinal authority which

Catholic teaching accords to him. They do not accept as binding the decisions of later Councils summoned by the Popes, though in fact the teaching of those Councils, for the most part, do not fundamentally conflict with Orthodox Church teaching.

Many other (mainly Protestant) Christians would claim that the Bible is the only real source of authority in matters of teaching. One of the slogans at the time of the Reformation was 'Scripture alone'. It was contended that the Scriptures were sufficient, and plain enough, though this did not prevent strong arguments among the Reformers over matters of doctrine. Some would allow some guiding role to basic decisions made by the Christian Church in the course of its history, and in particular would give at least some special authority to the early Councils of the Church. In practice, most Christian bodies accept the Creed as at least a summary of officially accepted fundamental beliefs. Variations in attitude make it difficult to be more specific without going into great and complicated detail.

The Place of Peter   [pp.241–243]
[p.242]   The quotation from Matthew (16:13–19) is a prescribed text.

Questions   [p.242]

1.   The powers of evil — which bring death — as opposed to the 'eternal life' brought by Christ.

2.   It seems to mean that Peter's authoritative judgments will be 'ratified' by God, or that he will make judgments with divinely given authority.

3.   It sinks, or breaks up. Because rock is firm and secure, and so supports what is built on it, and keeps it intact and steady.

4.   A position of high authority, and also the position of mainstay and support of the Church's unity and integrity.

[p.243]   The quotation from John (21:15–19) is a prescribed text.

Questions

1.   Three.

2.   Three.

3. He is perhaps giving Peter a chance to make amends for his threefold denial.

5. First 'Feed my lambs'; second 'tend my sheep'; third 'Feed my sheep'. There is a gradual build-up of the role he assigns to Peter. First only the lambs, then 'tending' the sheep (i.e. generally taking care of them), finally 'Feed my sheep', making him specifically responsible for their nourishment and health.

6. His 'sheep' are his 'flock', i.e. the Church. Peter is to give them the nourishment they need — the word of God and the Bread of life. He is to act as their shepherd in Christ's name.

The Pope   [p.243]
The Pope, the Bishop of Rome, is elected by the College of Cardinals. Nowadays, cardinals are senior bishops chosen from all parts of the world. At the time of writing, there are over 145 of them. In England the Archbishop of Westminster is traditionally made a cardinal, and in Ireland so is the Archbishop of Armagh. At present the Archbishop of Glasgow is also a cardinal. Apart from electing Pope, cardinals act as a special advisory body. According to the traditional reckoning, the present Pope, John-Paul II, is the 261st successor of St Peter.

Something to Do
Among 'Encyclicals' one may include here other Papal teaching documents, which though not technically classed as encyclicals, are rather like them. Some are technically 'Apostolic Exhortations'. Among the Encyclicals (or similar) of the present Pope are:

*   *Evangelium Nuntiandi* (on the sanctity of human life);
*   *Veritatis-Splendor* (on Christian life and morality);
*   *Redemptoris Mater* (on Our Lady);
*   *Familiaris Consortio* (on Family Life);
*   *Dominum et Vivificantem* (on the Holy Spirit);
*   *Redemptor Hominis* (on Christ, the Redeemer);
*   *Laborem Exercens* (on human work and related matters);
*   *Dives in Misericordia* (on Divine Mercy).

There are many others. Copies (in English) of many of them are obtainable from CTS.

Infallibility [pp.244–245]
This is a much misunderstood term. It does not mean sinless or perfect. It refers to a divine guarantee of *preservation from error*, and applies only in certain circumstances and under certain conditions.

The infallibility of Popes and Councils refers only to solemn dogmatic definitions, when the Church, using the fullness of its teaching authority from Christ, defines a doctrine concerning faith or morals as part of divine revelation, as something which is certainly and irrevocably part of that revelation, and which must be assented to in faith by all members of the Church. It is an occasion when the Church irrevocably 'nails its colours to the mast' for all time.

The central point of the doctrine of infallibility is that it embodies an assurance that a binding dogmatic definition by Pope or Council will not be allowed by God to be erroneous. It does not necessarily imply 'inspiration'. The Church believes that Pope and bishops enjoy the special guidance of the Holy Spirit, but that is not the same as saying that they are necessarily 'inspired' to make a particular pronouncement. The doctrine of infallibility does not say that Pope or Council is *necessarily* caused by God to make a certain kind of pronouncement, but that, if they do, one may be sure that God has preserved them from error. They do not receive and pronounce on new revelation, but define something concerning the meaning and interpretation of the revelation already made through Jesus Christ. The doctrine does not mean that their teaching on this point is as well expressed as it might be, or as full as it might be, or that it cannot be further elaborated or expanded. It simply means that it is in itself certainly true, and cannot therefore be ignored or contradicted. The foundation for the doctrine of infallibility lies not in confidence in the intelligence or virtue of bishops, but in the faithfulness of God, the promises of Christ, and the work of the Holy Spirit.

All dogmatic definitions by Councils require the assent of the Pope, as Head of the Apostolic College, for their validity. Any proposed definition which did not receive that assent would not be considered infallible.

In the history of the Church, infallible dogmatic definitions have usually been made when there has been dispute about some matter of faith, and when the Church felt the need to counteract what it considered to be erroneous doctrines. When there were no such fundamental disputes, dogmatic definitions were usually not considered necessary.

The Pope and Infallibility [p.245]
Though long widely held, the doctrine of papal infallibility was only solemnly defined at the First Vatican Council in the latter part of the nineteenth century. The Council established the conditions under which the Pope teaches infallibly. The doctrine was re-affirmed by the Second Vatican Council.

When it is said in the Student Text that none of the last four Popes has made an infallible pronouncement, that does not mean that what they have taught does not contain teaching which is infallible on other grounds. It simply means that none of them has made a certainly and explicitly infallible dogmatic definition.

Because the Pope does not usually teach infallibly, that does not mean that the rest of his teaching lacks force. On the contrary, the Second Vatican Council teaches that 'loyal submission of the will and the intellect must be given, in a special way, to the authentic teaching authority of the Roman Pontiff' (i.e. the Pope), and that this means that 'his supreme teaching authority be acknowledged with respect, and that one sincerely adhere to decisions made by him' (Vatican II, *Lumen Gentium* 25).

Questions [p.245]

1. Inspiration necessarily implies that God in some way *causes* someone to say or write something. Infallibility simply implies that he negatively *preserves* someone from error. In addition, in some contexts, inspiration may imply the communication of a new revelation. There is no such implication in the doctrine of infallibility.

2.   Through the decisions of Ecumenical Councils approved by the Pope.

3.   So that there may be certainty about the meaning and interpretation of the Christian faith, and so that the truth of the Gospel and the unity of the Church may be preserved.

13. *Ecumenism*   [pp.246–248]

Among the other Christian communities in England, Wales and Northern Ireland apart from the Catholic Church, there are: the Eastern Orthodox Churches, Anglicans (Church of England, Church in Wales, Church of Ireland), Methodists, Baptists, United Reformed Church, Presbyterians, various Pentecostal churches and the Salvation Army. (The list is by no means exhaustive).

A framework for ecumenical co-operation is provided by the organisation called 'Churches Together In England' and a similar body in Wales called CYTUN. The Catholic Church is a member of both.

The Catholic Church is not a full member of the World Council of Churches, though it sends observers, but it does take a prominent part in a number of its commissions. It also maintains in Rome the Pontifical Council for the Promotion of Christian Unity, headed by a Cardinal. Details (and addresses) of the ecumenical bodies in England and Wales may be found (among other places) in the National Catholic Directory. Details of diocesan provision for ecumenical activity and co-operation may also be found in the local Diocesan Directory. Pupils only need to know, in general terms, the main aims of ecumenism and have some idea of the general scope of ecumenical activity. They should also be able to appreciate the kind of difficulties which may arise, and have opportunity to develop their ideas on the value of ecumenical activity.

Course Work
One of the course work assignments must be concerned with some aspect of ecumenical activity or with some church community other than Roman Catholic. The latter of these options gives opportunity not only for Catholic pupils to become acquainted

with some other local Christian community, but also for Christian pupils of other denominations to do some work, if they wish, on their own church. In any case, it affords all pupils the opportunity to give some specific and fairly detailed attention to the life of a Christian community other than the Catholic Church.

With regard to the first option, it should be observed that the ecumenical activity or co-operation in question need not necessarily involve Roman Catholics, though it may well do. Contacts with local Christian church communities may well suggest a number of opportunities for working on an ecumenical topic. There may also be a specific institution or project, enjoying ecumenical support, which could itself supply a suitable subject.

Whatever choice is made, once again, teachers should first read carefully the guidelines and advice on Coursework contained in the Support Material supplied for this Syllabus by the Examining Board.

The Catholic Church and Other Churches
This sub-section outlines the Catholic view, as expressed by the Second Vatican Council. Other Christians would, of course, view the matter differently.

Catechism of the Catholic Church

The following are some of the articles from the Catechism which may be found useful in regard to topics dealt with in this Section.

Magnificat etc. (273, 722, 967, 2617–19); Mission of the Church (849–852, 857–859, 863, 1565); Sacraments (1113–1130); Baptism (1213–1274); Confirmation (1286–1314; Mass as Sacrifice (1337–1344, 1356–1372); Celebration of Mass (1345–1355); Holy Communion, Presence of Christ in the Eucharist (1373–1398); Ordained ministries (1554–1571); Lay ministry and apostolate (897–913); Consecrated Religious Life (914–933); Teaching Authority and Infallibility (75–90, 857–860, 874–890); Ecumenism (813–822, 836–838, 846–848)

UNIT 5

LIFE, MARRIAGE
AND THE FAMILY

Section A : Human Life

This Section deals successively with the topics detailed in the Syllabus content, and includes treatment of the texts prescribed in connection with these, as appropriate. In the outline given below, indication is given of the sub-sections in which *texts prescribed in the syllabus* occur.

Outline of Section A

1. *In the Image of God*
   Texts: *Gen 1:26–27*

2. *Respect for Human Life*
   Value of human beings
   Safeguarding and protecting life
   Texts: *Lk 10:27*

3. *Abortion*
   Background Information
   The Teaching of the Catholic Church
   Basic Questions
   Alternatives to Abortion
   The 'Hard Cases'

4. *Euthanasia*
   Meaning
   The Catholic Position
   The Point of Principle and the Slippery Slope
   Other Considerations
   The Alternative

The syllabus is open to all candidates, irrespective of religious beliefs, and therefore there is no presumption, in this Unit or others, that candidates will necessarily subscribe to particular views. In examination answers, where they are giving their own views, they will not be required to express agreement with, or to argue for, pre-ordained conclusions. It should be noted, however, that the syllabus does require of candidates an *understanding* of Church teaching on the issues in question.

This Section is concerned with the value of human life, and with the approach to specified issues in which one's estimation of that value is of particular importance. The aim should be to help pupils to examine critically the chief factors involved in coming to principled judgments on these matters, to understand the arguments involved and the importance of the underlying issues, and to promote in them a capacity for moral reasoning and discernment which goes beyond superficial sloganising or merely instant emotional reaction. In other words, it is an aim which goes beyond the mere articulation and elaboration of 'feelings', and is concerned with the development of powers of analysis and balanced understanding in regard to moral issues. Teachers may care to consult the *Preliminary Background Notes*, found in this Teacher's Guide on pp.121–127. These are concerned with the general principles employed in Catholic discussion of moral issues, and are meant as background information for teachers.

1. *In the Image of God* [pp.251-252]

This opening subsection is very important, as it lays the foundation for subsequent discussion.

In the first place, it should be realised that for Christians to talk about the value of human beings or human life is not to imply that other elements of the natural world or other living creatures are without value. In the account of creation in Genesis, we are told that God saw all that he had made, and 'it was very good'. What is meant is that, because of the kind of creature he is, Man (male and female) has an altogether special value and status. Man is not just one of the many species of animals on the earth, but is a very special kind of being, made so by God. In the Catholic view, all of man's natural gifts are related to his special status in relationship to God. The fundamental basis of his dignity is his vocation to share in God's life. It is because this is the reason for which he was created that he has been made the kind of creature who can be enabled to live in communion with God, to share his life. There is therefore in him a certain inbuilt likeness to God. In particular, there is that spiritual dimension, which is traditionally called 'the soul', and there is his status as a *person* — as *someone* rather than merely *something*. He is a free conscious personal subject.

The following articles of the *Catechism of the Catholic Church* summarize the position.

356 Of all visible creatures only man is 'able to know and love his Creator' (*Gaudium et Spes* 12,3). He is 'the only creature on earth that God has willed for its own sake' (*Ibid*. 24,3), and he alone is able to share, by knowledge and love, in God's own life. It was for this end that he was created, and this is the fundamental reason for his dignity.

357 Being in the image of God, the human individual possesses the dignity of a *person*, who is not just something, but someone. He is capable of self-knowledge, self-possession and of freely giving himself and entering into communion with other persons. And he is called by grace to a covenant with his Creator, to offer him a response of faith and love that no other creature can give in his stead.

364 The human body shares in the dignity of 'the image of God': it is a human body precisely because it is animated by a spiritual soul, and it is the whole human person that is intended to become, in the Body of Christ, a temple of the Spirit.

It is this idea of the human person as a free, self-conscious moral agent, capable of entering into communion with other persons, and above all with God, that indicates both the unique value of each human being and his status as someone 'made in the image of God.' Because he is, in the first place a *person*, a subject, the human being can ever simply be treated as an 'object'. Every human life must be considered of immense value, and be treated with the utmost respect.

Moral Agents
The concept of Man as free moral agent is very important. Human beings have much in common with other living creatures, but at the same time they stand apart from them in many ways. The

Student Text mentions a number of these — including rational intelligence and the corresponding capacity for a rich creativity. It is not just that human beings are more intelligent than animals; they have a different *kind* of intelligence, which enables them to form completed concepts, to engage in abstract thought and self-reflection. Above all, they have freedom, which makes them not only capable of creative initiatives but of truly moral decisions and moral acts. Sometimes, especially nowadays, animals are favourably compared to human beings. However, observations of this kind miss the point. Creatures which lack freedom will act in accordance with the most powerful instinct. In reality they are neither to be praised or blamed, in a moral sense, for their actions. It is only human beings, who are capable of free choice and free decision, who are truly moral beings. They alone can be the agents of moral evil (but also of moral good). Human beings may debate whether it is *right* to hunt foxes. Foxes not only do not, but *cannot* debate whether it is right to hunt rabbits.

Incidental Questions
Should the question of the relationship of human beings to the rest of the created world arise, material may be found on pp.183–184 of the Student Text. Treatment of animals in particular is briefly dealt with on p.172. Teachers are reminded, however, that the subject of 'animal rights' as such does not form part of the syllabus content of this Unit.

Things to Do
[p.252]

1. Some mention of some or all of: rational intelligence, creativity, freedom, personhood, spiritual.

2. Only in a very limited sense, particularly not in the sense of personal relationship and the sharing of life and love freely on a personal level.

3. A variety of possible answers. All will involve some expression of selfishness, irresponsibility, lack of love, lack of respect for God's creation, for other people etc.

2. Respect For Human Life [pp.253-254]

The first paragraph of the Student Text draws out the implications of the previous subsection. If human beings are valuable in themselves, their fundamental value may not be assessed on other criteria. To do so is to reduce them to the category of objects. Each person is valuable in himself/herself, irrespective of any contribution made to society. The value of a human person is not something determined by other people. It is intrinsic.

It is worthwhile considering the possible implications of opposing views. Taken to a logical extreme, they may lead to approaches and practices such as those found in Nazi Germany, where the handicapped were considered simply 'useless mouths', who should be, and often were, eliminated.

Resect for human beings and human life, however, does not merely imply avoidance of homicide. It implies an attitude of respect and consideration for the dignity of every human being, and concern for safeguarding and protecting human life.

The syllabus specifically mentions 'the value of handicapped people', and this topic is briefly dealt with in the Student Text. This treatment could be profitably illustrated and expanded by reference to concrete issues, organisations etc. This area might furnish the basis for a useful coursework assignment. There might, for example, be some local institution, association or activity which could provide a subject for investigation by pupils.

A brief introduction to 'ways of endangering life and safeguarding life', as mentioned in the syllabus, is given in the Student Text, but again this could well be illustrated and broadened through the use of current or local specific examples, which are best provided by the teacher, or suggested by the pupils themselves.

Safeguarding and Protecting Life [p.254]
With regard to the list of actions given here, the 'simply stupid' one is, of course, 'Lighting a match to look for a gas leak'. All the others involve some degree of recklessness or lack of sufficient concern for the lives of others (and of oneself). Each should be discussed in turn.

Additional Activities

1.   Design a poster or a display to illustrate the following:

ALL PEOPLE ARE VALUABLE!

WHO SAYS SO?

GOD SAYS SO!

2.   Sometimes, often unintentionally, handicapped people can be treated patronisingly or as though they were less human or less important than others.

EITHER   Write a short story in which this happens.

OR   Act out a scene in which this kind of thing occurs.

3.   In groups, design posters warning against a variety of ways in which people can endanger the lives of others. The title for the whole display is:

PROTECT HUMAN LIFE

3. Abortion   [pp.255-262]

(N.B. In some early printings of the Student Text, in the caption to the photograph on p.255, the organisation LIFE, by the accidental use of the definite rather than the indefinite article, is apparently erroneously equated with 'The Society for the Protection of the Unborn Child'. The Society with that name (SPUC) is, of course, a different organisation, though both it and LIFE oppose abortion.)

Background Information   [pp.255–257]

The passage on what is here meant by abortion seeks, above all, to make the point that what is being discussed in this subsection is direct and deliberately intended 'termination of pregnancy'. It is concerned, in other words, with 'induced' or 'procured' abortion. In some medical works the term 'spontaneous abortion' may sometimes be found to describe what are more popularly and usually described as 'miscarriages'. These are involuntary events, not deliberately brought about. They are not what is meant here by 'abortion'. On the other hand, deliberately to bring about a 'miscarriage' in order to secure a lethal 'termination of pregnancy' is itself a method of 'induced' or 'procured' abortion. An 'induced miscarriage' of this kind therefore is in fact equivalent to an 'induced abortion'. It is included in what is here meant by 'abortion'. In brief, 'abortion' is here meant to designate any procedure deliberately designed to secure the death of the unborn child at any stage.

Grounds for Abortion [p.255]

The legal situation described here applies only to Great Britain. The situation in Northern Ireland is very different. There are wide-ranging variations in abortion law in countries throughout the world. In some countries it is still illegal. In others it is very strictly limited. In others there is literally or virtually abortion on demand.

Age Limit on Abortions [p.256]

It appears that there is particular scope for securing a very late abortion on the grounds that the unborn child is suffering from some handicap.

Methods of Abortion

Only a very general outline is given of possible methods. The point about the abortifacient effect of certain 'contraceptive' pills/drugs is an important one. The point is that the effects mentioned are not contraceptive. They do not prevent conception, but act on the already conceived human embryo. What is destroyed therefore is a new, distinct, individual human life in its initial stage, a stage through which every human individual passes. It is therefore a true abortion.

Basic Facts about Human Life before Birth [p.257]

It is presumed that pupils know that a child is conceived through the fusion of one of the father's sperm with an egg (ovum) from the mother. Some, however, may have strange or inaccurate notions about the nature and growth of the child in the womb, and the outline of the process of gestation is included both to supply general information, and to enable pupils to appreciate that the child in the womb is a distinct individual from the earliest stage, one which rapidly develops in a recognisably human form, and which is clearly alive. It also may help them to envisage what abortion at various stages involves. Visual support material may be obtained from one of the organisations mentioned below.

Additional Literature, Information, Teaching Aids etc.
Details of videos, slides, pamphlets, charts and other literature on
the development of the child in the womb, and/or on abortion
specifically may be obtained from:

- LIFE, LIFE House, Newbold Terrace, Leamington Spa,
  CV32 4A; tel. 01926 421587.
- SPUC, 7 Tufton Street, London, SW1P.
- Human Life Education, 32 Ravine Road, Bournemouth,
  BH5 2DU.

LIFE and SPUC will usually be glad to supply or recommend a
suitable speaker and/or visual presentation on these and related
topics. In addition to material specifically or exclusively concerned
with this area, the last part of the Video *The Three R's of Family
Life*, later recommended in Part B of this Unit, may also be found
useful. It is available for purchase or hire from: Family and Youth
Concern, Wicken, Milton Keynes MK19 6BU. (It may also be
hired from: Maryvale House, Old Oscott Hill, Kingstanding,
Birmingham B44 9AG; tel. 0121 360 8118.)

The Approach to Discussing Abortion
The material in the Student Text tries to encourage the
development of an objective, principled view, not one that is
merely an emotional reaction. Emotions can be powerful spurs to
involvement and positive action, but one must be sure that they are
adequately based. They can rouse us from moral lethargy, but they
can also, if not properly scrutinized and regulated, cloud our
judgment. It is not enough to find abortion aesthetically or
emotionally repugnant. It may be considered aesthetically and
emotionally repugnant to amputate someone's diseased leg, but it
may nevertheless be both necessary and justifiable to do so. The
question about abortion is not whether it is 'nice', but whether it is
'right', whether it is 'just'.

The fundamental argument against abortion which is suggested in
the Student Text is the one which underlies almost all pro-life
protest on this matter. The argument is that abortion is the
deliberate taking of innocent human life; it is therefore massively
unjust and gravely wrong. To deprive someone of life is to deprive
him/her of all other rights. This is therefore an argument about

basic justice, about basic human dignity and the most fundamental of human rights; it is about unjust discrimination of the most extreme kind. This is, of course, an issue that will arouse strong emotions in those who see it in this light, though it is an argument which prompts strong emotions, and though these emotions may well arouse people to active involvement in moves to oppose the practice in question, it is not in itself a merely emotional argument. The case against abortion is in fact not well served, if it is treated in a purely emotional way.

The Teaching of the Catholic Church [p.258]

The Student Text gives a brief outline of the basic teaching. More extensive treatment of the matter may be found in *Catechism of the Catholic Church 2270–2274*. Among other Church documents which the teacher may care to consult are:

- John-Paul II, *Evangelium Vitae*, 1995;
- Congregation for the Doctrine of the Faith, *Declaration on Procured Abortion, 1974*;
- Bishops of England and Wales, *Abortion and the Right to Live* (CTS S345).

The list of 'values at stake', given in this part of the Student Text, starts with the basic consideration of the right to life, but then goes on to indicate other highly important areas for which the issue of abortion has serious implications. Each of these give rise to various questions. For example, most people accept that parents have duties to protect and nurture their children. They are not allowed to kill them once they are born, if they prove to be a burden or inconvenient. Moreover, we expect parents to be naturally protective of their offspring, and to accept responsibility for them. Does not the acceptance of abortion stand in contradiction to all this? Is it not a refusal of care, a denial of protection, and abandonment of responsibility? Is it not undermining the whole concept of parenthood, and encouraging highly dangerous attitudes? The unborn child is the child of his/her parents just as much as the child who is born. Equivalent questions may be asked in respect of mothers in particular and the idea of motherhood, and in respect of the attitude of doctors. In general, the question might be asked: is not the acceptance of abortion corrosive of attitudes and relationships over wide areas of human life? There should be thorough discussion of each of the 'values' listed.

Basic Questions about the Unborn Child [pp.258–259]
The Catholic Church teaches that, if an act is wrong in itself, it cannot be justified by a good end. Therefore, if abortion is in itself wrong, no good purposes or claims for the benefits it may bring for others can justify it. However, even for those who would accept that, at least in some circumstances 'the end justifies the means', there is still some difficulty about justifying abortion on the grounds of the burdens or difficulties it removes from the mother, the family or others, if at the same time it is still accepted that what is 'terminated' in an abortion is truly a human being. Not only must one face the difficult question of whether, in a choice between the welfare of one human being and the actual life of another, the taking of that life (and with it all the rights that depend on it) can ever really be considered as 'the lesser of two evils', one has also to face up to the fact that the implication of what one is saying is that in certain circumstances it is all right to put innocent people to death.

Very often, therefore, those who support abortion do not merely point to the burdens that can be removed by the termination of an unwanted pregnancy, but argue in addition that, in any case, the unborn child is in some way not really human or not fully human or a person. The Student Text gives a representative sample of such arguments and the counter-arguments commonly advanced against them. This is a key issue in this subsection.

Situation — Philip and Abortion [p.259]
The situation may raise all kinds of reaction, both principled and 'pragmatic'. All should be thoroughly discussed. This situation deliberately focuses on Philip, to emphasize that this kind of situation is not simply the woman's problem. Philip has problems here, but does he also have responsibilities — to the girl, to the child? In some cases girls are pressurized by their boyfriends to have abortions. In such circumstances whose interests are being put first? A wide variety of questions can emerge from discussion

of a situation of this kind, especially if it is sensitively guided by the teacher.

Teachers could well devise other situations for discussion on this general topic, or devise role-play scenarios for groups of pupils.

The 'Hard Cases' [p.261]
These are called 'hard cases' precisely because a decision against abortion may involve particularly severe consequences for the woman involved, and perhaps for her family as well.

That consideration should certainly engage everyone's sympathy and concern, but does it alone decide the matter? Christians would generally agree that doing what is right is not always easy. Often it will involve difficulties, and sometimes very painful and trying consequences. One cannot decide what is right simply by calculating what is to one's own benefit or convenience. Catholic teaching would say that, though the consequences in these cases may indeed be burdensome and worthy of every sympathy and all the support that may be given, nevertheless one cannot for that reason simply eliminate an innocent human life.

It should be made clear, however, that the question is: 'Is abortion right or wrong in such circumstances?' rather than 'Should one stand in condemnation of those who have abortions in such circumstances?' Most people, whether they oppose or support abortion, will have considerable sympathy for and emotional engagement with those who find themselves in such a predicament, and will be loth to appear to stand in judgment upon them. In itself this is entirely understandable, and indeed thoroughly Christian. Christians are told not to stand in judgment on others. But it may also interfere with their readiness to consider the moral question in an objective manner. it may perhaps impel them totally to subjectivize the issue, saying something like 'It all depends how they feel about it', or 'It is their decision'. Such reactions, however, simply evade the moral issue. A decision to do something does not in itself make it right or wrong. How someone feels about something may tell us about his/her sincerity, but not necessarily about the rightness or wrongness of his/her act. Christians should not stand in judgment on others, but they must judge what actions are right and what actions are wrong.

The central question remains. If the unborn child is truly human, can it simply be put to death?

The case of abortion of handicapped children deserves particular attention. What does this say about the perceived value (or lack of it) of handicapped people? How far are economic considerations, on the part of the state, involved in all this? Many would consider the particular emphasis on facilitating the abortion of children likely to be born with handicap particularly disturbing. Why?

4. *Euthanasia* [pp.263–265]

This subsection is specifically concerned with euthanasia, of which assisted suicide is an aspect, and therefore the ethics of suicide can properly be considered within its remit. The whole topic does also, of course, incidentally raise wider questions concerning medical ethics and the responsibility of preserving one's own and other people's lives.

The treatment given in the Student Text is relatively general in tone and content. It needs to be supplemented and illustrated by concrete examples. A number of these crop up regularly in the news media, and teachers should be alert to collect them. In doing so, however, they should ensure that they are prepared eventually to present these to a class in a way which enables pupils to identify the principles and arguments involved, and to engage in a critical analysis of a situation which may sometimes be presented in a one-sided, simplistic or over-sensationalised manner. It should be appreciated that some of the media specialise in 'gut reaction', but that such reaction is not always the safest or wisest guide.

Because some situations may involve complex technical and medical details, teachers should seek to focus discussion mainly on the matters of principle involved. In some cases the adoption of certain principles will clearly demand a particular course of action; in others, their precise application, and the course of action they demand, may depend on as yet unresolved answers to certain questions, and so will allow only a provisional or conditional judgment. In order to help pupils to identify arguments and basic points of principle at issue, teachers would be well advised to choose, at least in the first instance, relatively straightforward cases.

Meaning and Kinds of Euthanasia [p.263]

Though the question of non-voluntary euthanasia is passed over quickly in the Student Text, since it is not the principal focus of the current debate, one should not suppose that, as yet, it is a merely abstract or theoretical question. There have been in Europe in recent years publicly proved cases in which an institution terminated the lives of elderly patients, initially, it is said, to end their sufferings, but eventually to dispose of them when they became too much of a burden. In England, a few years ago, an old people's home, becoming suspicious of the activities of relatives of one of its inmates, arranged for a TV crew to record secretly what went on between them and the old lady in question. What viewers witnessed was a clear attempt by relatives to pressurize the old lady into ending her life. Quite obviously there could be many instances where people might have a definite interest, financial or otherwise, in the death of an elderly relative.

Nor is non-voluntary euthanasia concerned only with the old. Very recently a British doctor publicly stated that some years earlier, completely on his own decision, he had given a lethal injection to two severely handicapped babies. It is not to be supposed that he is the only one. In addition, there is the practice of euthanasia by omission of appropriate care or treatment, rather than by positive lethal acts. In this country, there is a growing practice whereby doctors, with the parents' consent, heavily sedate new-born handicapped babies, so that they do not demand feeding, and consequently die. A recent court case indicates that in certain circumstances even the objections of close relatives may be over-ridden. In the case of an adult, Tony Bland, who had long been in a profound coma, the courts allowed doctors to withdraw all feeding of the patient, despite the objections of Tony Bland's mother. In effect, the court appeared to be sanctioning euthanasia by omission of basic care.

In Holland, where voluntary euthanasia, supposedly under certain strict conditions, is widely practised, there is evidence of a considerable occurrence of non-voluntary euthanasia as well. In the Hemmelink Report, published in 1991, a survey was mentioned which revealed that, in the case of 5,450 patients, doctors had pursued a course of either positive actions or of omissions with the explicit purpose of shortening life, *without the explicit request* of the patients concerned.

Euthanasia by Commission or Omission

As mentioned above, euthanasia can be performed by the omission of care or treatment, as well as by, for example, a lethal injection. A recent report by a select committee of the House of Lords came out strongly against euthanasia (a fact widely welcomed by those campaigning against its introduction), but defined euthanasia mainly in terms of positive acts, and gave little detailed attention to the question of euthanasia by omission. This is, however, a very important aspect of the problem. One can kill someone just as effectively by denying him/her basic care or nourishment as by administering positively lethal treatment. Euthanasia is an act or an omission chosen with the aim of ending a person's life. It normally involves the judgment that this life is without value, or is not worth living.

Common Arguments for Euthanasia

Arguments for euthanasia typically follow the following lines. It is said that people, especially those with terminal illnesses or in great pain, have a right to die with dignity, when they choose, and that it is inhumane to seek to deny them this right. It is further said that the legalisation of such a right, and the consequent empowerment of medical personnel, under suitable safeguards, to perform lethal acts, is consequently a merciful and desirable measure, and that to oppose it is to condemn countless people to years of undesired indignity and/or suffering. The power of this argument lies not only in the fact that most people, quite naturally shrink from suffering themselves, but that they are also distressed by the suffering of others.

Another related factor, especially as it relates to the cases of handicapped infants, those in a comatose state and the elderly whose mental faculties are notably impaired, concerns 'quality of life'. Has the life in question any point or value, either for the person concerned or for others? Allied to this, there is often the consideration of the economic cost to families or the state of caring for such people, and of other burdensome consequences or distress for relatives.

Overall the contention, and justification, tends to rest on the consideration that, for one reason or another, the life is not (or is no longer) of value, or is not worth living.

The Catholic Position   [p.264]
Basically Catholic teaching opposes euthanasia (and suicide):

- because it involves a claim to a degree of dominion over human life which human beings do not possess, but which belongs to God;
- because it offends against the fundamental dignity and intrinsic value of the human person and of human life.

Euthanasia strikes at the heart of that duty of care which we all owe to others, and which is especially owed by medical personnel to their patients. In cases of non-voluntary euthanasia, it is a particularly gross infringement of the fundamental human right to life.

In addition to what is said in the Student Text, a few other observations may be made. In the first place, it should be realised that Catholic teaching does not encourage Christians to cling on to life *at all costs*. Christians have to be ready to sacrifice even their lives for the sake of what is right and to be prepared to suffer death rather than to perpetrate evil. To sacrifice one's life to save others is rightly regarded as a noble act. Nevertheless, life is a gift of obviously fundamental importance. To be prepared to lose one's life in a good and worthy cause is one thing. Deliberately to take one's own life is quite another. The right to life is similarly fundamental. Taking that away automatically involves taking away all other rights as well.

Catholic teaching holds that all have a duty to take reasonable care of their own life and health, which they receive as a gift from God. They also have a duty to defend and safeguard the life of others, and certainly to avoid all reckless or deliberate endangerment or infringement of other people's right to life. They may not co-operate in another's suicide, or take another's life, even at his/her request. The value of a human life and of a human person does not depend on the value others put upon it, nor even on the value placed on it by the person himself or herself; it is intrinsic. It has value in itself.

Doctors in particular have a duty to do the best for all their patients, in the circumstances that exist and within the limits of the resources available. In no circumstances may they perform or omit any procedure *with the intention* of bringing about or hastening the patient's death. According to Catholic teaching, however, a doctor is not obliged to use extraordinary or too excessively burdensome means artificially to prolong life or the dying process, nor is a dying patient obliged to accept such treatment. There comes a point when doctors may simply accept their inability to prevent death, and simply ensure that the patient is given ordinary care and nourishment.

According to Catholic teaching, it is permissible for a doctor to alleviate severe pain in a dying patient, even if it is anticipated that the treatment may hasten his death, as may happen with the use of morphine. At first sight, it may seem that there is no real difference between this and a lethal injection, but there are in fact important distinguishing factors.

- In the case of a lethal injection, the intention of the doctor is to bring about death. This is euthanasia. In the other case, the intention of the doctor is simply to alleviate pain, with the possible hastening of death merely an undesired by-product.

- The intention of the doctor will be reflected in his approach to the treatment in question. The one who intends to bring about or hasten death will ensure, above all, that he gives what is certainly a lethal dose. The one whose aim is merely to relieve pain will be careful to give only what is necessary for that purpose, and carefully avoid a directly lethal dose.

The moral principle governing this approach is the *Principle of Double Effect*. An explanation of this may be found in this Teacher's Guide on pp.123–125.

Further information on Catholic teaching on this matter may be found in *Catechism of the Catholic Church* (2276–2283).

It is worth mentioning that, although we have been talking here of the Catholic position on these matters, it is one which is in substance shared by very many other Christians. Some of the foremost opponents of euthanasia in America, this country and the rest of Europe are non-Catholic Christians.

The Point of Principle and the Slippery Slope [p.264]
The argument concerning life as a gift of God and God's dominion over life cannot, of course, be expected to carry much weight with an atheist. Nevertheless there are many with no particular religious beliefs who appreciate the central argument that to move away from the idea of the sanctity and intrinsic value of all human life would be a highly dangerous and morally corrosive step with incalculable consequences. Current experience already points to the kind of trends which the legalisation of even voluntary euthanasia might enormously exacerbate. Would it not end in a vastly altered attitude towards human life and human beings in general?

Already it is obvious that, though some arguments are concerned with the liberation of patients from suffering, others are concerned more with the interests of others — relatives or even the state — rather than with those of the patient himself. It can be argued that in many cases euthanasia is being proposed, not because life is intolerable for the person concerned, but because he/she is considered to be a burden on the family, state, health service, social services etc. What value, it might be asked, is being given to human life and the human person here?

One may also question the concept of 'quality of life'. Who is to decide what is the minimum 'quality of life' which somehow makes a life valuable, or whose lack deprives it of value. If we draw up a list of qualities or capacities which a human being must have or be able to exercise, if his life is to be considered of value, we must ascribe a higher moral status progressively to those with greater and greater capacities. The lives of the less intelligent would have to be considered less valuable, and consequently more readily disposable, than those of the more intelligent. The notion of the fundamental equality in dignity among human beings would depart.

Two general implications of basing a decision to end someone's life on the grounds that his/her life has no value are drawn out by Helen Watt of the Linacre Centre, London in her paper *Euthanasia — Some Moral Aspects* (obtainable from: LIFE, LIFE House, Newbold Terrace, Leamington Spa CV32 4EA).

> 'If the patient's life is of no value,... then it is hard to see why the practice of euthanasia should be confined to terminal cases. If the patient's life has no value, it may surely be terminated, whether the patient is dying or not. The second consideration is that if the patient's life has no value, but the patient is unable to consent to euthanasia (being unconscious, or mentally handicapped, or senile, or simply too young), it is not clear that there is anything to stand in the way of our killing that patient, at least if the relatives give their consent. It is therefore not surprising that many supporters of voluntary euthanasia also support (whether openly or discreetly) non-voluntary euthanasia. For if death is either a benefit, or at least no harm, why should we deny it to those who cannot request it?' (p.5)

This indicates the path on which acceptance of voluntary euthanasia might set society, and the dangerously subversive nature of some of the grounds used to justify it. One might add that it is worth considering what the effects might be on the medical profession and on society generally of encouraging doctors to view death as a 'benefit' or as a species of 'care'.

The Medical Profession   [p.265]
The ancient Greek physician, Hippocrates, formulated an oath, the *Hippocratic Oath*, to govern the conduct and attitude of doctors. It is still taken by many doctors in various parts of the world. One of its key principles is the protection of life and the avoidance of any harm to the patient. A modernized version was drawn up in Geneva in 1948. Part of it runs as follows:

> 'I will maintain the utmost respect for human life, from the time of conception; even under threat I will not use medical knowledge contrary to the laws of humanity.'

Pupils might be asked if they think anyone could observe this oath, and at the same time perform either abortions or euthanasia.

The Alternative — Hospices   [p.265]
The Irish Sisters of Charity founded the first hospice in Europe in the nineteenth century. In the twentieth century the work of hospices has greatly developed, especially through the efforts of Dame Cicely Saunders in England.

A hospice and its work could form an excellent subject for a coursework assignment.

Further Information on Euthanasia

- The pamphlet by Helen Watts, *Euthanasia — Some Moral Aspects*, is available from: LIFE, LIFE House, Newbold Terrace, Leamington Spa, CV32 4EA (tel. 01926 421587).
- Information may also be available from: ALERT, 27 Walpole Street, London, SW3 4QS (tel. 0171 730 2800); and from SPUC, 7 Tufton St, London SWlP.
- A good book for background reading is: L. Gormally (ed.), *Euthanasia, Clinical Practice and the Law*, Linacre Centre, 1994.

Catechism of the Catholic Church

The following articles may be found useful in respect of Catholic teaching on the various topics in this Section: 355–367, 2258–2291.

Section B : Marriage and the Family

This Section deals successively with the topics detailed in the Syllabus content, and includes treatment of the texts prescribed in connection with these, as appropriate. In the outline given below, indication is given of the subsections in which texts *prescribed in the syllabus* occur.

Outline of Section B

1. *Love*
    Particular expressions of love
    Jesus on Marriage
    Commitment, fidelity, union, self-giving
    Marriage and children
    Marriage as a Sacrament
    Everlasting love
    Texts: *Mk 10:2–12; Eph 5:25–32; 1 Cor 13:1–13*

2. *Getting Married*
    Marrying young
    Preparation for marriage
    The Catholic Rite of Marriage

3. *The Family*
    Duties of Parents
    Marriage and Society

4. *Divorce*
    The Divorce Rate
    The Catholic Church: Separation and Divorce
    Information on annulment
    Texts: *Mk l0:2–12*

5. *Sex Outside Marriage*

6. *Family Planning*
    Artificial Methods and Natural Methods
    The Ethics of Birth Regulation: Catholic Teaching
    Advantages and Dangers

1. *Love* [pp.266–274]

This subsection is about the interconnection of love and marriage. It begins with an analysis of love, which should be thoroughly discussed with pupils. The key distinction is between real love and mere attraction. (More on a similar theme may be found in Unit 3, pp.150–151 of the Student Text.) The Student Text here deals successively with friendship, parental/filial love and 'romantic' love. It then goes on to deal with love specifically in connection with marriage.

Additional Exercise
With regard to the material on pp. 266–267, pupils might be asked:

1. Do you know, or can you find out the meaning of: 'cupboard love', 'fair-weather friendship'?

2. Write a story in which someone discovers who his/her real friends are.

Something to Do [p.269]
The exercise suggested here can be very useful. The aim is to help pupils to read such literature critically, and to discern implicit assumptions and values, hidden agendas etc. As an introduction, teachers may care to read *The Seductive Sell*, ed. Joanna Bogle (Family and Youth Concern, Wicken, Milton Keynes, MK19 6BU).

Jesus on Marriage
The quotation from Mark (10:2–12) is a prescribed text.

Questions (first set) [p.270]

1. 'God made them male and female.'; 'For this reason a man shall leave his father and mother and be joined to his wife.'

2. He speaks throughout of 'wife' in the singular, and of 'two' becoming 'one'.

3. 'They are no longer two, but one flesh.'

4. 'What God has joined together, let not man put asunder.'; 'Whoever divorces his wife and marries another, commits adultery against her....'

Questions (second set)

1.   'things don't go well';
     'we/you become less well off';
     'we/you become ill or disabled'.

2.   Selfish attitudes generally, lack of real commitment to the
     other person, entering marriage only for what one can get out
     of it personally.

The mention of lack of freedom and exclusion of permanence as
grounds for annulment in the last paragraph on p.270 is primarily
intended to underline the importance of these factors as necessary
aspects of a true marriage.

Questions   [p.271]

3.   They pledge themselves to each other 'in an unbreakable
     alliance of total mutual self-giving'.

Marriage and Children
The student Text tries to make clear that:

• openness to the gift of children is an intrinsic and necessary
  feature of what the Catholic Church considers to be a true
  marriage, to the extent that the deliberate exclusion, at the time
  of marriage, of the intention to have any children would render
  the marriage null and void;

• this only applies to deliberate exclusion of what would
  otherwise be possible; couples who, through the infertility of
  one or other party, are in fact incapable of procreating children
  may still validly marry.

The procreation and upbringing of children is in fact considered a
prime purpose of marriage, and forms part of the normal marriage
vocation.

This treatment of Marriage and Children, together with the
following material on *Marriage as a Sacrament* (pp.272–273) can
well form the basis for discussion of marriage as a *vocation*. The
vocation is twofold:

• to grow together in love, and so to be a sign of Christ's love in
  the world, and more able to be a source of love for others;

- especially to bring new human beings into the world, and to bring them up in an atmosphere of love, which reflects the love of God.

  'Married couples should regard it as their proper mission to transmit human life and to educate their children; they should realise that they are thereby co-operating with the love of God, the Creator, and are in a certain sense its interpreters.' (Vatican II, 'Gaudium et Spes' 50).

Marriage as a Sacrament [pp.272–273]
The quotation from Ephesians on p.272 is a prescribed text.

Questions [p.273]
1. By saying that it is to be like the love for the Church shown by Christ who 'gave himself up for her' — a reference to the Crucifixion.

2. By saying that husbands should love their wives as their own bodies.

3. He means that the two are so closely united that for a husband to love his wife is like loving part of himself. He has the same kind of care and concern for his wife and her welfare and happiness as he has for his own, because now they are completely bound up with each other.

Everlasting Love [pp.273–274]
The quoted passage from 1 Corinthians is a prescribed text.

Questions [p.274]
1. A variety of possible answers: because it is love which shapes our real intentions and attitudes, because love is the basic Christian commandment, because to love is to be like God, because love is God's greatest gift, etc.

2. Patient, kind, rejoices in the right, bears all things, believes all things, hopes all things, endures all things.

3. Not jealous, arrogant, rude, does not insist on its own way, not irritable, resentful, does not rejoice at wrong.

4. Eventually faith will not be necessary, because we will see God face to face; eventually hope will not be necessary,

because we will have achieved our destiny. But, since we will live in a relationship of love with God for ever, God's gift of love will always be necessary, and will be eternal.

Videos
Teachers may care to consider using the following videos:

* *The Three R's of Family Life* (in three parts: 1. Respect Yourself; 2. Respect your partner; 3. Respect Life), available for purchase or hire from: Family & Youth Concern, Wicken, Milton Keynes MK19 6BU.

* In connection with marriage and/or subsection 4 on divorce, the Video, *Staying Together*, available from Human Life Education, 32 Ravine Rd, Bournemouth BH5 2DU

* In connection with marriage and/or with subsection 5 on sex outside marriage, *When, Jenny, When?* and *Girl on the Edge of Town* (both Paulist Productions).

All the above videos are also obtainable from Veritas. They are also all available on hire from: Maryvale House, Old Oscott Hill, Kingstanding, Birmingham B44 9AG (tel. 0121 360 8118).

2. *Getting Married* [pp. 274–279]

One aim of this subsection is to help pupils realise that marriage is a serious matter, that it should be approached responsibly, and prepared for. There should be careful discussion of the question of 'marrying young', and the implications and lessons of the statistics.

Preparation For Marriage
This is an item specifically mentioned in the syllabus. Pupils need to know, in general terms, about the kind of preparation that might be expected before a Church wedding, but they need not know all the details given on p.276. Neither do they need to know the details of the legal requirements given on p.277, which are merely included for further information. They need only know that there are legal formalities involved, including the granting of a licence or certificate by the Registrar. What is chiefly important is that they should have thoroughly discussed and formed opinions upon questions concerning the considerations which should underlie

entry into marriage, and the nature of a sensible preparation for marriage. The kind of questions included under *Discuss* on p.277 are particularly important.

The Catholic Rite of Marriage   [p.278]
Again, acquaintance with the nature of the Catholic Marriage service is specifically mentioned in the syllabus. The details given in the Student Text are quite sufficient. In section B of the outline of the service, certain words are given in bold type. In each case these correspond to certain central features of the Catholic understanding of marriage.

Discuss   [p.279]
Pupils are asked to comment on the special significance of these words. The following notes indicate the main points.

- *freely* — The essence of marriage is free consent. Without it, there is no marriage.

- *give yourself* — Marriage is essentially a commitment, a self-giving of one to the other. It is more than a mere contract.

- *for the rest of your life* — Marriage is essentially for life. It is a permanent state.

- *accept children* — The openness to the gift of children is an essential feature of a true marriage. The procreation of children and the founding of a new family is a prime purpose of marriage, which cannot be deliberately excluded.

3. The Family   [pp.280–282]

Catholic Teaching on the Family is outlined in the *Catechism of The Catholic Church* (2201–2233). The teacher would be well advised to consult these articles. In this subsection and the next, the question of the breakdown of marriage, and the consequent fragmentation of families, is brought up. Teachers should, in their approach, be sensitive to the home conditions of their pupils.

Discuss   [p.280]
1.   Company, ready-made companionship, conditions which encourage learning to share, co-operate, etc. Many others could be added.

2. Loneliness, the danger of being spoiled, of becoming selfish, etc.

3. Sometimes the youngest may be treated more indulgently, which causes jealousy and resentment, but it all depends; it could be the other way round.

4. They tend to behave more carefully. They are not so free and easy. Because it is not their home. They do not have the same 'rights' there.

5. Perhaps what is lacking is the sense of personal 'belonging'. It is the security of feeling part of a lasting set of relationships, bound together by lasting bonds, to which one belongs permanently and by right. It is also concerned with the need for a child to have the personal and unconditional love and nurture of a father and a mother figure, which is seen not just as something temporary and transient but a permanent constant feature of life.

6. Probably because it gives them a basic sense of security, of being wanted and of being valued. It helps them to feel at home in the world and enables them in their turn to show love and affection to others.

7. No good parent would give a child what was harmful for it, or allow it to risk needless danger. Nor would a good parent encourage a child to become too self-centred or selfish.

Duties of Parents   [pp.280–281]

Questions (first set)   [p.281]

1. It may shatter their sense of basic security. Children may also be torn between the two parents. They may greatly miss the parent who leaves the home, and this may have a very disturbing effect on them.

2. The responsibility of making very sure they do everything they can to safeguard their marriage.

Background Reading
Teachers may care to consult one or more of the following studies of the importance of the family unit, and the consequences of widespread family breakdown:

- R. Whelan, *Broken Homes and Battered Children* (Family Education Trust, 1994);
- N. Dennis and G. Erdos, *Families Without Fatherhood*, (IEA Health and Welfare Unit, 2nd edn, 1993);
- N. Dennis, *Rising Crime and the Dismembered Family* (IEA Health and Welfare Unit, 1993).

The treatment in this subsection concentrates mainly on the importance of the family for children, but, of course, it is also important for people of all ages, and perhaps especially the old. Some attention could well be given to this aspect.

4. *Divorce* [pp.283–286]

The statistics given on p.283 are no doubt rather alarming. They are supplied in order to give some idea of the extent of the problem and of the number of people affected. At the same time, one should not be too negative or pessimistic. While a great many marriages fail, most in fact last. There is no inevitability about divorce.

Pupils should discuss the contributory reasons suggested for the increased divorce rate. Which do they think are the most important, and about which do they think something can most readily be done, both by individuals and by society as a whole?

Discuss [p.284]

1. There could be a great variety — for example, difficulty in adjusting to one another, constraints of no longer being independent, problems with one or other of the families, housing difficulties, financial difficulties, etc.

2. Among the reasons may be the fact that the birth of a child drastically changes a couple's life. Looking after a baby can be tiring and time-consuming. It also puts limitations on other activities. Parents may feel 'tied' to the house because of the baby. Income may fall if a wife gives up her job. The husband may feel neglected. There may be disputes if all the work is left to one partner, etc. The main safeguard probably is advance awareness of likely problems, advance planning, where possible, to lessen them, and a readiness to talk and

listen to each other, and to seek available help from families, etc.

3. Debatable, but it may make it more tempting to take what might seem an 'easy' way out, rather than trying to overcome the difficulties.

4. Could be many reasons. Such behaviour might indicate a lack of readiness for commitment, make it difficult for someone to adjust eventually to a permanent faithful union. It could indicate a casual attitude to the significance of sexual relations which would make him/her less likely to take marital fidelity seriously, etc.

5. Perhaps feeling the need for a trial marriage was a sign of lack of real commitment to each other in the first place. Compatibility is not the same as commitment, nor is it a substitute for it or for a proper attitude to the meaning of marriage. Perhaps after living as though married for a time, marriage itself seemed a bit of an anticlimax.

The Church: Separation and Divorce   [pp.284–285]
The information on separation is included to make clear that the Church does not insist on people (especially women) continuing to endure intolerable or dangerous treatment from their spouse. The position on divorce is simply that a true marriage between Christians is for life, and can only be dissolved by death. It is not that the Catholic Church refuses to grant or recognise divorce as part of Church discipline, but that it believes that it has no power to do so.

The information on p.285 seeks to emphasize that it is not the mere fact of a civil divorce in itself which necessarily excludes a Catholic from Communion, but the contracting of a second 'marriage', while the first partner is still alive. The Catholic Church believes that civil divorce does not cancel out the first marriage, which remains in force. However it accepts that in some cases there may be legal reasons which make it advisable for someone to go through divorce proceedings, while accepting that this does not in fact dissolve the marriage. In addition, of course, there are many people who have been legally divorced against their will. Even some Catholics wrongly believe that such people, simply because they are 'divorced', may not receive Communion, but that is simply not true. The decisive factor is the question of a subsequent 'marriage' or cohabitation with another.

An exposition of Catholic teaching on the indissolubility of marriage, and on divorce, separation etc., may be found in *Catechism of the Catholic Church* (1639–1640, 2382–2386). The video *Staying Together* (Human Life Education — see notes at end of subsection 5) may also be found useful.

Annulment
The question of nullity is not specifically mentioned in the syllabus. Some outline understanding is, however, necessary, in order properly to appreciate Catholic teaching on divorce, and it can provide a useful way of underlining what, in the Catholic view, constitute the real essentials for a true marriage.

Pupils do not need to know all the details given on p.286. These are given for extra information, and to illustrate the fact that annulment is concerned with something that was not a true marriage in the first place.

Pupils need to know the basic difference between divorce and annulment.

- *Divorce* is a procedure by which an already existing true marriage is brought to an end.
- *Annulment* is a declaration that what looked like a marriage was never a true marriage from the beginning.

They should also know a few straightforward examples of grounds for nullity. About three would be enough. One would suggest that the obvious ones are those which have previously been mentioned in the Student Text:

- *Lack of freedom* — Free consent is essential to marriage. Without it there is no true marriage from the beginning.
- *Exclusion of permanence* — Marriage is essentially a union for life. To enter a supposed marriage without the intention that it is for life is not to enter marriage at all, but an essentially different arrangement. Therefore from the beginning there is no true marriage.

- *Exclusion of offspring* — A prime end of marriage is the procreation and upbringing of children. To enter a supposed marriage with the deliberate intention of *avoiding* having any children contradicts the purposes of marriage. Therefore there is no true marriage from the beginning.

There are, of course, other obvious cases which one could use, but these are relatively straightforward, have already been mentioned in regard to other matters, and are good illustrations of some important aspects of the Catholic understanding of the nature of marriage.

5. Sex Outside Marriage [p.287]

The central point is that, according to Catholic teaching, sexual relations are intended by God for marriage and nowhere else. Outside marriage they involve a grave misuse of God's gifts which is likely to have a range of destructive consequences. The approach given here is relatively straightforward, but could well be supplemented with others. Outlines of other complementary approaches may be found in the Archdiocese of Birmingham *Family Life Education Project*, Second Year Booklet, available from Maryvale House, Old Oscott Hill, Kingstanding, Birmingham B44 9AG (tel. 0121 360 8118). More developed versions of some of these, together with other relevant material, may be found in *A Time To Live*, Book 3 of 'The New Christian Way Series', published by Veritas. See especially pp. 275–279. Some good basic ideas are contained in a short pamphlet: *But Where Is Love?* by Venetia Riches, obtainable from Family & Youth Concern, Wicken, Milton Keynes MK19 6BU. Obtainable from the same source, there is also a useful leaflet, *Saying No*, which contains some good points for discussion.

Videos
The following may be found of use:

- *The Three R's Of Family Life* (especially section 1), obtainable from Family & Youth Concern at the above address;
- 'When, Jenny, When?' (Paulist Productions).

The point of the remarks about taking 'precautions' on p.287 of the Student Text is that, even if one adopts an amoral 'pragmatic' point of view, the activity is still irresponsible, because such 'precautions' not infrequently do not work. From a Catholic point of view, however, that is, of course, not the fundamental objection, which is that the activity is in any case wrong. The argument here is that, even from the viewpoint of those who do not accept Catholic or general Christian teaching, it can be seen as a hazardous and irresponsible action. (See note on the failure rate of condoms in the subsequent material on Family Planning in this Guide).

A concise account of relevant Catholic teaching may be found in *Catechism of the Catholic Church* (2351–2356, 2380–2381).

6.   *Family Planning* [pp.288–292]

Artificial Methods
The outline details given here are sufficient for the purposes of this subsection. A number of these methods have side effects and possible dangers associated with them. For example, mechanical methods can cause vaginal bleeding and other complications, quite apart from the fact that they are really abortifacients. Hormonal methods can contribute to the danger of thromboses, strokes, etc., and are associated with an increased risk of cancer of the cervix.

The 'failure' rate of condoms is considered high. A recent survey showed that the bursting or slipping off of a condom had occurred to no fewer than 52% of the sample of experienced condom users over a three-month period (*British Journal of Family Planning 1990*; 15: pp.107–111).

Further concise details of contraceptive methods, their characteristics, drawbacks and dangers, may be found in the Archdiocese of Birmingham, *Family Life Education Project*, Upper School Booklet (pp.43–47), obtainable from Maryvale House, Old Oscott Hill, Kingstanding, Birmingham B44 9AG (tel. 0121 360 8118).

Natural Methods
A brief outline of Natural Methods may be found in the *Family Life Education*, Upper School Booklet, detailed above. There is also a CTS pamphlet *Natural Family Planning* (CTS S350).

If teachers wish to obtain a suitable, well-informed speaker to talk further about this area, Natural Family Planning Clinics and certain other bodies concerned with the same area will usually be glad to supply or recommend a suitable person.

Contact Addresses
- NFP Service, 1 Blythe Rd, London W14 ONW will be able to supply you with details of services which exist in your area.
- NFP Centre, Birmingham Maternity Hospital, Queen Elizabeth Medical Centre, Birmingham B15 2TG.
- The CMAC, if one exists in your area, may also be able to help.

Book
A useful detailed book for background information is *The Billings Method* (Gracewing, 1994).

Ethics
Natural Family Planning respects the order established by God, respects and maintains human fertility, encourages mutual respect, consideration and co-operation between spouses, has no hazards or dangers. These are some of the reasons it is accepted by the Catholic Church as legitimate and useful. It is moreover, as recent research has shown, highly reliable. It also can be used to facilitate as well as to avoid pregnancy. In the Catholic view, it is in accordance with the dignity of the human person and the dignity and importance of marital sexual relations.

Catholic teaching on this whole Matter may be found in *Catechism of the Catholic Church* (2366–237). Teachers might also care to consult:
- Paul VI, *Humanae Vitae*;
- John-Paul II, *Familiaris Consortio.*

Both of these are available from CTS.

Catechism of the Catholic Church

The Sacrament of Marriage (1601–1666), the Family
(2201–2233); divorce etc. (1639–1640, 2382–2386); sexual
morality in general (2331–2400).